WOMEN AND MICROCREDIT

WOMEN AND MICROCREDIT

By

Dr. M. Lakshmi Narasaiah
M.A., Ph.D.,
Professor and Head
Department of Economics
Sri Krishnadevaraya University
Post-graduate Centre,
Kurnool—518 002
Andhra Pradesh

SONALI PUBLICATIONS
NEW DELHI-110002

First Published-2004

ISBN 81-88836-27-3

Published by

SONALI PUBLICATIONS
4228/1, Ansari Road,
New Delhi-110 002 (India)
Phone: 23279245 • Fax: 91-11-23253475

Printed at: Tarun Offset Printers, Delhi-53

PREFACE

Over half the people in the Indian Community are Women. The change in Women's Contribution to society is one of the most striking phenomena of the late twentieth-century. But although, they have had the law behind them, women have yet to enjoy the equality they are entitled to in theory. Men need to contribute more to family life, while women have yet to make a real impact on decisions affecting the lives of everybody.

Technological advances have meant the decline of employment in manufacturing, and the growing dominance of service industries. This has meant more jobs for women, but not necessarily better working conditions. Most women are still in lower-paid jobs, 'and most still work mainly with other women in similar jobs and fields. Women are still under-represented in many sectors of industry, the professions and public service.

More and more women are involved in paid work. There is no job they cannot do, and they are entitled to equal pay for equal work, as well as the same terms and conditions at work, and the same opportunities for promotion. Giving women the opportunity to realize their potential in all spheres of society is increasingly important, for all only by involving both sexes to the full can we develop human resources on really democratic lines.

Author

CONTENTS

1

WOMEN IN AUTHORITY
(The Ideal and the Reality)

At the current rate of progress it will take a very long-time to bring about equality in sharing decision-making between men and Women in all areas. In terms of human rights and social justice, such equality is absolutely vital; it is also the best way to promote change with a human face. Would the world be a better place if women had equal access to management positions.

A NEAR ABSENCE

Almost everywhere in the world, Women have the vote and account for over half of the electorate. With but rare exceptions, however, their political activities are restricted to anonymous and informal roles in local communities. They hover at the margins of the higher levels of trade union, political, Governmental and corporate life, and of interest groups. Until 1987, women occupied rarely 10 per cent of parliamentary seats. The same holds true for the trade unions, despite the fact that women account for nearly one-third of union memberships. Indeed, the Women to have reached the leadership of a trade union can be counted on the fingers of one hand. This pattern of inequality is mirrored, indeed accentuated, in the employers' organizations, where Women are practically absent. Everyone knows the situation in professional employment. Women continue to be concentrated in lower-qualified, lower-paid jobs, and very few manage to attain managerial posts, though the trend is on the increase.

LOWER-PAID JOBS

The "invisibility" of women in public life, and consequently in political, economic and professional activity, is both the cause and consequence of their being consistently barred from positions of authority. The way in which cultural and social models repeat themselves creates a setting that is hardly conducive to women progressing much beyond the limits of their homes and immediate working and living environment. Enmeshed in a tangle of little encouragement and probable reprobation, women are hesitant about struggling to advance in professional or political careers, as to do so would frequently put at stake the subordinate role that hitherto atleast guaranteed them a secure position within the family circle." On the other hand, as they hardly manage to participate fully in the decisions affecting their lives and families, it will prove difficult for them to break out of the vicious circle.

RIGHTS AND OBSTACLES

Why is it then essential for women to play an equal role in decision-making? One can approach this objective from three points of view. First, it is a clear question of human rights: women make up half the population and more than one-third of the work-force and so their right to full citizenship and equality of opportunity and treatment in employment must be clearly expressed by their participating in all levels of activity. Secondly, it is a matter of social justice to combat discrimination against women, which is at its very harshest when it comes to employment. Thirdly, it is an essential requirement for the acceleration and effectiveness of development, as women are capable of providing a different sort of ability and creativity, which has not so far been tapped, and they can ensure a better balance in the allocation of resources and distribution of the benefits of progress.

TWO TYPES OF OBSTACLE

There are two types of obstacle to be overcome in order that women can have access to decision-making positions—structural and situational. The include the famous differences in levels of education, occupational experience and income levels as compared to men. These combine with and are reinforced by the situational factors such as the burden of family responsibilities, legal, psychological and material dependence on their spouses and male relatives, colleagues or bosses, and the fact that society is not prepared to change its attitudes and support women in assuming positions of responsibility. The deeply rooted "gender ideology" underlying all this constitutes a system of barriers to the upper echelons. It takes the form of values, attitudes and behavioural patterns which inhibit development and the recognition of the leadership qualities of women and which thus demand additional sacrifices from those who nevertheless strive to overcome them.

ADDITIONAL SACRIFICES

It has been estimated that women's participation in excess of 30 per cent in the upper echelons would be necessary for any noticeable difference to be made to the nature and tenor of the decisions taken in the areas affected. So what would this difference be? Women tend to speak with a "different voice" which as a rule lays stress on the social ethos of development, that is to say education, health, children, environment, dialogue and peace. Conversely, men tend to concentrate on the economic aspects such as production, trade, profitability, finance, technology and national defence. If we really aspire to any development of the human lot involving both economic growth and social equity, the best way to achieve this coveted objective will be by having men and women sharing in decision-taking.

2

EQUAL OPPORTUNITIES FOR WOMEN IN THE COMMUNITY

Over half the people in the Indian Community are Women. The change in women's contribution to society is one of the most striking phenomena of the late twentieth-century. But although, they have had the law? Behind them, women have yet to enjoy the equality they are entitled to in theory. Men need to contribute more to family life, while women have yet to make a real impact on decisions affecting the lives of everybody.

Technological advances have meant the decline of employment in manufacturing, and the growing dominance of service industries. This has meant more jobs for women, but not necessarily better working conditions. Most women are still in lower-paid jobs, "and most still work mainly with other women in similar jobs and fields. Women are still under-represented in many sectors of industry, the professions and public service.

More and more women are involved in paid work. There is no job they cannot do, and they are entitled to equal pay for equal work, as well as the same terms and conditions at work, and the same opportunities for promotion. Giving women the opportunity to realize their potential in all spheres of society is increasingly important, for all only by involving both sexes to the full can we develop human resources on really democratic lines.

EQUAL PAY, EQUAL OPPORTUNITIES

The right to equal pay for equal work without discrimination based on sex has to be set out. Equal treatment in access to employment, training, promotion and working conditions has to be encouraged. Equal treatment in social security, as well as for the self-employed are very much needed. Rights to maternity leave and pay, and a guarantee of adequate health and safety at work for pregnant women and nursing mothers are very urgent. The Government has to encourage good practice on: Positive action, vocational training, child-care, combating unemployment, equal opportunities in schools, integrating women into working life, combating unwanted sexual behaviour at work, education, and updating protective legislation affecting women. There is still a great deal to be done before we can claim women in the community really get a fair deal and a chance to show what they can do.

Women are still often segregated into jobs that are less well-paid than those typically taken by men. They are often well qualified than men, and the jobs they do are often less secure. These are the kinds of inequalities the society must continue to combat and it will do so, as one of the ways of making sure women do not bear the brunt. Quality and quantity in women's employment is very important.

BETTER OPPORTUNITIES TO EARN A LIVING

Getting more women into paid work by promoting job opportunities, entrepreneurship and local employment should be the aim. The aim should be to help them fulfil their potential through better education, training and positive action. Upgrading their skills and equipping them with hi-tech know-how is a priority. Another major concern is helping parents juggle work and caring responsibilities via better services and terms of employment.

GETTING WOMEN IN POSITIONS OF POWER

It is hard to believe over half the community's population is female, given how little direct influence women have over what happens in our society. In an electoral constituency where half the voters are women, and where concerns for education, family health and food are paramount, both contestants up for election are male, and they speak to a largely male audience. The Women, who work long hours and worry and sacrifice for their families and homes, fuss with the tea, hush the children, over on the periphery. If they are there at all. Politics is 'men's business'.

Training to Keep up with the Times

Women need training if they are to benefit from growth and technological development. A network of training schemes, have to be set up to develop training for women, to publicize their needs, promote information exchanges and encourage the involvement of employers and trade unions.

Changing Minds in School

There is no job women cannot do. A working party is looking at ways of encouraging boys and girls to range more widely in the subjects they take in school. It should aim to support teachers trying to avoid reproducing anachronistic stereo-types.

Pregnant women, mothers of newborn babies and nursing mothers should have the peace of mind of knowing they have secure health and social rights. For women who already have to combine their professional life with running a home and looking after children, political activity requires considerable sacrifices. Women would be more ready to take them on if they thought they stood a chance of recognition on a par with men. That is far from being the case. If equal opportunities for women are provided definitely the country will develop at faster rate.

3

WOMEN IN POLITICS

The Participation of Women in political life today on the agendas of most political parties in India However, attempts to translate this goal into concrete reality have had limited success. A basic reason for this is the lack of conceptual clarity about the genuine commitment to the issue. For any such endeavour to be successful, it must be recognised that the equal participation of women and men in decision-making in all spheres is a prerequisite for effective democracy.

Participation means more than female membership in political parties, female voter turnout in elections or a token female presence in political bodies. Participation must be meaningful and effective, and must include representation in the political arena. This includes not only formal or higher level decision-making forums, but also other political units: the family, community groups associations, trade unions and local bodies. These are crucial areas for intervention within which women can easily understand the issues and play an effective role.

The identification of barriers to Women's Political Participation is obviously a prerequisite for overcoming them, but the visible barriers do not necessarily reflect the 'entire situation, and are often merely indicative of more deep-rooted problems. Governments tend to address the issue by devising measures capable of showing quick results. But tackling visible barriers without addressing their root causes results at best in temporary success.

Overcoming the barriers means not only eliminating them but also ensuring women's participation through other means. Affirmative action measures should not be perceived as privileges or concessions, but as interim measures to reverse existing imbalances, until such time as genuine equality and parity is' achieved.

India must review its policies, constitution and legislation to see whether these have been discriminatory towards women, or have been ineffective in promoting women's rights. Since the issue of women's participation cannot be addressed in isolation, one must identify and assess factors affecting the development of a democratic culture or the recognition of human rights concerns. These factors include the country's political history, its socio-cultural, ethnic and religious diversity, the impact of traditional, customary, feudal and tribal laws, and the use of religious interpretations regarding women's rights.

One must review the prevalent general situation of women. While inequalities and imbalances exist in all places some have stronger patriarchal structures wherein gender roles are more rigidly assigned. It is particularly important to assess women's political participation, including political-rights, participation in election process and political parties, representation in legislative bodies and local councils, women in the civil service and in trade unions, and women's groups and lobbies.

Barriers to Women's Political Participation can be legal, social, financial or political. In addition to identifying such barriers, it is useful to assess initiatives taken by Governments and Non-Governmental Organisations (NGOs), to evaluate successes and failures, identify the reasons and make modifications.

Based on the above, appropriate multi-pronged strategies and actions must be devised. It is important to develop a clear policy articulating the effective involving of women in the formulation of laws and policies which govern their lives.

Measures must be taken to ensure the principle of equality as a fundamental right. National Legislation must be amended or repealed to remove any discriminatory provision. Positive legislation must be introduced to promote or protect affirmative action measures. The language of the law must clearly address itself to men and women, changing the practice of using the legal 'he' to include 'she'.

Research must be undertaken to cover information gaps. Monitoring mechanisms, guidelines and indicators must be devised and a process of periodic data collection established, to assess changing trends. Documentation and analysis of innovative initiatives must be ongoing, to help in devising and modifying strategies.

Women's human rights and power sharing issues must be integrated in all training programmes of Government, semi-Government and autonomous institutions. Key personnel involved in decision-making and implementation need to be made sensitive to gender issues. Political education and training programmes for women are needed at the community level, for NGOs and community-based organisations, communicators, development workers and media personnel, etc.

Campaigns to change attitudes and social norms and project a positive image of women can be run through educational efforts and the media, and public discussions and debates. A clear stand should be taken against any misrepresentation of religion which stands in the way of women's equality and political participation.

Workshops and seminars should promote closer interaction between women in NGOs, advocacy and research groups, Government departments, political leadership, trade unions, worker's associations and the media.

A minimum quota should be established for women in all sectors and grades of the civil service, including Government, semi-Government and autonomous organisations. A minimum percentage of key advisory positions, directorships, etc., should be reserved for women. Advertisements for Government jobs should specifically state women's eligibility.

Electoral rolls should be systematically updated to include all eligible women. Education should be provided on electoral rights, political parties, election issues and concrete ways of holding candidates and political parties accountable. Political parties should publish their positions on women's rights issues, and encourage women to vote on issues that concern them. Constitutions of political parties should exclude provisions which condone or justify discrimination.

An adequate minimum representation of women in legislative bodies and local councils can be ensured by reserving seats through such means as putting women's names in priority positions on lists, providing financial support to female candidates, and making legal provisions that only those parties which give certain minimum number of tickets to women are eligible to contest elections.

A Government Ministry with the requisite authority should be designated as a focal point for devising policy, ensuring implementation and coordinating with other ministries and agencies.

An autonomous Permanent Commission on the Status of Women should be set up to function as a think-tank on women's issues, to commission policy research and to review recommend and monitor the implementation of policies and Programmes in the field of development, rights and political participation. The Commission should comprise Government representatives, NGOs, human rights organisations and experts in different areas.

A judicial authority should expedite Women's human rights cases; this could take the form of a human rights bench, a tribunal or an equality ombudsman. These are only some of the basic principles and 'guidelines that can be adopted. Ultimately, however, no strategy can be effective unless it is also backed by the requisite political will and impetus.

4

EMPOWERMENT FOR WOMEN
(The Gap Between Theory and Practice)

Actually, the situation of women has changed completely in the last 30 years. At the beginning of the 1970s women were a blind spot in both development aid and the debate on it. The promotion of women is now established in all state institutions and Non-Governmental Organisations (NGOs). Gender training is to sensitive development workers to take a gender specific approach in analysing development processes, carrying out statistical surveys, and planning and evaluating activities.

FROM INTEGRATION TO EMPOWERMENT

Those women who in the 1970s criticised development policy and its actors for being one-eyed must now see themselves as line-prompters and idea-providers. All the terms they used have been adopted in official usage. The image of the woman has changed from being a Cinderella-like, hard-done-by person, the poor soul, the victim, to a dynamic, reliable actor with apparently inexhaustible reserves of energy and creativity to bring to bear in a development process that has got stuck. The concept of empowerment has replaced the old "integration in development" approach in the promotion of women. And the women's approach (Gender and Development). This calls for the inclusion of men, taking a close look at the gender relationship and changing it into the long-run.

All this undoubtedly progress which illuminates the blind spot. So is that enough to please women critics of the male-dominated development aid scene and female lobbyists for the promotion of women? Have they achieved what they wanted? That is, a policy on women which on the one hand takes up their practical, everyday needs, but on the other works strategically towards eliminating the hierarchy between the genders by structural changes? The fact is that one must differentiate between what Governments, multilateral institutions and NGOs are saying and what they are doing.

REDISTRIBUTION OF SOCIAL POWER AND CONTROL OF RESOURCES

The empowerment concept makes clear the political and economic gap between men and women, it aims at a redistribution of social power and control of resources in favour of women based on a Development Strategy' which is no longer oriented on growth, the world market and military power.

The concept has had seemingly record acceptance in the executive suites and programmes of the Governments while at the same time its substance has been drastically diluted. Taken on board hook-line-and-sinker by official-policy, its politically critical teeth-namely posing the power question—have been extracted. It now has no bite critical of development and social-policy. It just stands modestly and harmlessly for every strengthening and participation of women.

Professionalization on the NGOs side and state orientation on the grass roots have brought activities nearer to one another. The modes of expression are identical. But where are women really at the centre of development practice? And where are they at the centre of developmental organizations? The promotion of women is still an appendage to development policy, including in most NGOs. That is shown not only by the low number of "pure" women's projects, but also by the subordinate role of women's interests and measures for women in integrated programmes. Defined as a "cross-sectoral task", the advancement of women is often reduced to the mere addition of a women competent. For example, in the form of small-scale loans for sewing machines. The few women in the organizations are assigned a low-ranking and sparsely-equipped niche.

Lack of Long-Term Strategy

The gender approach has made the yawning gap between rhetoric and practice even bigger. It might be useful as an instrument of analysis, if it is not debased to a technocratic checklist. But no-one at present knows for sure how it can be implemented. The international trend is to implement promotion of women less in "pure" women's projects than to integrate it in other activities. Parallel to that, there are signs of a trend in which the women's or gender sections of development agencies are being disbanded and integrated in country or specialist sections. Currently, however, there is apparently still a lack of concepts for implementing a strategically oriented advancement of women. If integration, or "mainstreaming", now takes place at the various levels, it is to be feared that the promotion of women will peter out rather than spread.

At the same time, disenchantment prevails among those who have understood that the advancement of women is a means to more rights and opportunities in life, more self-confidence and social recognition. The demand to effect structural change through projects founders on the general conditions. Like development assistance as a whole, raising the status of women is also in many regions becoming increasingly merely disaster relief and survival aid. All involved have long known there are no universally applicable formulas for projects, and still fewer handy "directions for use" for getting out of poverty and blasting open patriarchal suppression.

The dilemma is clear. The economic crisis, the over-indebted and socially inactive Governments, and the men who steal away from responsibility are saddling women with ever increasing burdens in securing survival. Thereby the women urgently need support. At the same time, the limited impacts of promotional measures, or even their boomerang effect, and becoming more obvious.

Many women are being catapulted into the exploitation mechanisms of the market and money economy only when they get involved in projects. Or, at least, the projects are speeding that process. Because of the projects the women neglect subsistence production and their traditional principles of the moral economy. But it is also clear that as a result of training programmes, new forms of organization, development of new fields of action, and mobility, women's groups would collapse.

Thus, the old dilemma—of here a policy of small steps necessary for survival, and there big strategic and structural concepts-has got worse. But there's no way around it: the advancement of women must continue to seek bridges between being content with little and the vision of a development that is more just to women.

5

WOMEN AND POVERTY

It is becoming more evident that the majority of the poor in developed and developing worlds are women. Poverty among rural women is growing faster than among rural men. Over the past 20 years, for example, the number of women in absolute poverty rose by 50 per cent as against some 30 per cent for rural men. The alarming evidence concerning the underlying trends for this process strongly indicates that the gender composition of the poor is veering towards a greater share of women.

Poverty manifests itself in many ways among migrant and refugee women, elderly women and children and indigenous women. Poverty is a complex, diverse and dynamic condition stemming out of depravation with respect to income, from social inferiority, isolation, physical weakness, powerlessness and humiliation.

Analysis of women's poverty suggest that its main causes stem from the perpetual disadvantage of women in terms of their position in the labour market, access to productive resources and income for the satisfaction of their basic needs. They also demonstrate that poor women possess exceptional resourcefulness, initiative and entrepreneurial spirit and that they show tenacity and self-sacrifice in trying to take a long-term view of their poor economic conditions and in safeguarding their livelihoods.

Development is the most important challenge facing the human race. The lack of progress in the last twenty years in the eradication of poverty and growing proportion of women among the poor is the single most important threat to the progress of development and its sustainability. As long as three-quarters of the world population continue to suffer from acute depravation, as long as profound imbalances in global consumption continue to persist, and, more important, as long as the spread of poverty, particularly among women, continues unchecked, there can be no development. The history of the development process shows again that the economic status of women is the key variable in the solution to the poverty crisis. It is time for the full recognition of the fact that women are part of the solution to poverty and to the stagnating development, not part of the problem.

The Earth Summit in Rio, the Human Rights Conference in Vienna, the population Conference in Cairo and the Beijing conference all were milestone events in terms of advancing our understanding of the crucial role of women in development and focusing the attention of the international community on the issues concerning the role of women in the work place and in society. All of them drew attention to women's full and effective participation in development. None, however, full articulated how to achieve this challenging task.

It is important to retain focus on the issue of economic potential when discussing poverty among women because it is clear that power is only meaning something in practical terms if it is reinforced by economic power. Women have the means to transform productive resources into such power if only enabling environment is created. It is not the lack of capabilities, but that of resources which is clearly responsible for women's poverty.

Sometimes, the so badly needed resources are not even truly scarce. Billions have been wasted on arms purchases around the globe and particularly in the countries which can not afford such misallocation of public funds. At the same time, women's organizations from grassroots to the international level are poorly funded. Such misallocation of resources at the time when poverty among women is increasing, is immoral and unacceptable, not only on the part of the Governments which pursue such wasteful policies, but also on the part of the suppliers, who in most cases are developed economies.

Government's responsibilities do not end here. It is extremely important, and indeed it is the main duty of every Government around the world, to provide a conducive environment for economic growth and stability by pursuing responsible and sound micro-economic policies which will enable the economy to grow without marginalizing women. When inflation is rampant, when political climate is unstable, leading to conflicts and civil strife, little can be done for poverty alleviation.

6

LIGHTENING THE LOAD FOR WOMEN

Not only do women in India suffer greater poverty than men, they often have little choice but to pass it on to the next generation. Investing in women, therefore, is an effective way of building a better economic future for the poor.

Research findings from all sources are confirming what development practitioners have long observed: women are generally worse off economically than men, and the consequences of their poverty are more serious for future generations.

Women's poverty differs from that of men both in degree and in kind: women experience greater poverty and transmit their disadvantage more readily to their children, thus, perpetuating the poverty cycle. At the same time, however, they are better able than men to protect children from the consequences of poverty.

It is this close connection between women's and children's fortunes that makes women's poverty a prime target for enlightened development practice. Anti-property policies need to reach poor women both to maximize social return on development investments and minimize the poverty of this and the next generation.

BREAKING THE POVERTY CYCLE

Poor women's rising participation in the world of paid work, however, does not necessarily guarantee a destiny of poverty. On the contrary, their earnings can protect children from poverty. Until fairly recently, the prevailing assumption was that any positive income effect of women's employment on children's health and well-being would be offset by negative effects of reduced child care time by working mothers or by the substitution of older siblings in child care. Recent studies, however, indicate a positive effect of women's employment on child health and nutrition. Women prefer to invest meagre earnings on child well-being and underscore the point that the income poor women earn can yield higher social benefits than income earned by men.

These positive effects of poor women's income-earning activities are not necessarily contradictory with the negative effects of women's increased work on their daughter's educational opportunities. It is likely that women need a minimum level of income to act on their preference to invest scarce resources on child-well-being below which their additional work perpetuates rather than halts poverty.

POLICY AND RESEARCH IMPLICATIONS

It is therefore desirable to implement policies that reinforce the virtuous cycle between women's and children's well-being that can occur in poor families when women have more income, and avoid those that can instead trigger a vicious cycle of deprivation between mothers and children. Circumstances which increase poor women's unpaid or very low-paid work can foster the perpetuation of disadvantage. These include the effects of declining household incomes during economic downturns, the decrease in service provision by the State which accompanies Structural adjustment programmes, and many community and child-centered interventions that rely heavily on women's unpaid time. Anti-poverty packages need to reinforce poor women's roles as economic producers and avoid actions which increase women's unpaid labour for the promotion of family child welfare.

Projects which increase women's productivity in home and market production and expand their employment options can help to turn the vicious cycle of poverty into a virtuous one. This necessitates executing agencies which can work with women, and budget allocations to strengthen the capacity of institutions to implement and monitor gender—responsive employment programmes for the poor.

The reach of project interventions is restricted, however. Their impact is often short-lived and while they can help to contain the cycle of poverty between mothers and children, they cannot in themselves transform women's economic activities. Changes in the policy environment are required for the latter. These include agricultural policies which target poor farmers and give women farmers access to land, credit and technical assistance; financial policies which promote the growth of small enterprises and foster entrepreneurship among women; and labour-intensive "pro-poor" economic growth policies. In addition, Governments need to invest in upgrading women's occupational skills, and in a series of complementary measures, including overhauling social security systems, establishing gender friendly regulatory frameworks for agricultural and industrial growth, and legislate on child care options.

To guide these policies, we need: research that distinguishes families from households and seeks to understand the formation, structure and dynamics of families headed by women; longitudinal studies which provide a narrative for events in women's lives and assess the transmission of disadvantage between mothers and children; trend data which tracks changes in women's work as a result of changes in economic conditions and in implementation of economic and social policies; and analyses of the mechanics, costs and consequences of targeting interventions to female heads of households and poor women.

The policy-oriented research agenda is perhaps as ambitious as the policy agenda and both require funding. Investing in women should be an effective use of scarce development resources if these actions are guided by the basic principle of seeing women in India for what they are: Economic and social agents and not merely passive recipients of welfare.

7

PROMOTION OF WOMEN

Women made up more than half the World's Population, produced 80 per cent of its food, laboured for two-thirds of its working hours , were paid 10 per cent of its income and owned one per cent of its property.

These figures conceal manifold forms of the disadvantaging and discrimination of women. Such as the unjust division of burdens in families, the economic exploitation of women, the loss of their control over resources, and finally the unequal rating of paid and unpaid work. The latter, in the form of work for the family, on the land, for the community towards improving local living conditions, and nursing the old and the sick, adds up mostly to a 14-16 hours working day. True, employment of women has increased further everywhere in the world. But a number of them work in unsafe and socially unsecured conditions. They are also poorly paid and as a rule have hardly any chances to better themselves. Many women can earn money only in urban informal sectors or farming.

GLOBAL PUBLIC FOR WOMEN

To be sure, the Decade of the Woman (1976 to 1985), the adoption of the convention on eliminating every form of discrimination against women (1979), the key role of women in the development process and their rights have created a global public for them. Moreover, their activities have got underway a reorientation of international policies on women. But, despite numerous progressive international moves in the area of formal legislation, the political debates on the legal status of women are in no way over.

Making general statements on the correlation of the impacts of social development and the situation of women is difficult because the political, economic and cultural frame work conditions differ greatly from one country to another. However, discrimination against women manifests itself in most traditional as well as modern societies as a structural feature. Nowhere in the world are women treated "as good" as men, and all countries slip on the scale of human development when inequality between the sexes is measured. Differences between the life situations and opportunities of men and women still arise from unequal possibilities of access to employment, income, economic resources, health care, food, education and training.

Social developments such as fundamental changes in traditional family and social structures, migration, urbanization, the contrast between traditional and "modern" ways of life, and often unfavourable economic developments for the majority of the people have a great influence on the role of the woman in the Various Third World Countries. Moreover, the increasing differentiation of the South in terms of poorer and richer countries cannot obscure the fact that in the 1990s the general social conditions for the majority of women have not improved.

Almost one-third of all the people in the countries of the South live in life-threatening poverty, and the overwhelming majority of those are women. Female poverty has different aspects, such as poverty of income, low literacy, a lack of vocational training and the poverty of old age.

Further more, the continuing legal pluralism in many societies impedes efforts to achieve equality of status for women. Although, in many countries men and women are meanwhile equal according to the constitution and legislation, there is still a great contradiction between constitutionally guaranteed rights and reality. According to religious law or custom, women in many countries are not equal to men. That means they have no property rights, or may not sign and contracts without their husbands' and constitutional rights, this implies the danger of becoming poor, particularly for single mothers, divorcees or widows.

Against this background it is no surprise that women are under-represented at political decision-taking levels, in Government posts, political parties, trade unions and associations. The structures of many institutions give little support to women's interests, and managerial positions are held almost exclusively by men. In part, women-specific measures are seen as a compulsory exercise and, at best, tolerated as a fad.

NEW OPPORTUNITIES

But in general the radical changes taking place in many countries open New Opportunities for policies on women. On the one hand, this is because the extent of the disadvantaging and suppression of women is more visible. And on the other, because the fields of work for women have become wider—if mainly in urban centres. In some countries, women have been able to push through binding legal regulations (election laws, political party statutes, women's quota rules for local councils), in order to guarantee their stronger participation in parties and trade unions. With the programme slogans of "empowerment" and redistribution of power", Women who are organized in self-help organizations, associations, networks and political parties are demanding participation in political decision processes and access to the political institutions. They are striving for social power in a bid to influence the factors which cause discrimination against them.

The transition from authoritarian to democratic forms of Government in a great number of countries have placed women's organizations in a changed environment. There are now countless such bodies, and their combined clout is changing the status of women and helping to broaden their scope for social action. But in some countries women are still faced with considerable difficulties in organizing themselves with formal status.

On account of progressive impoverishment, however, the women's newly-son scope for action and shaping their lives is markedly cramped. Current developments such as religious fundamentalism or economic recession have inhibiting impacts on new approaches to policies on women in part, one must speak of a "backlash". Even where the legal position of women have been improved they have not been able to assert their social, economic and political rights. In some countries, it's feared that only elitist women's organizations will have a chance to break into the political process.

8

POPULATION GROWTH AND WOMEN'S ROLÉ IN INDIA

We have limited economic resources. There is a pressing need to abolish poverty. If population grows unchecked, abolition of poverty becomes very difficult. Due to the rise in population, illiteracy is growing as educational facilities are not expanding as fast as the population. Though employment facilities are being provided, we are not able to solve the unemployment problem. Though, production and national income are rising, standard of living is not rising at the same rate. Thus, growing population remains a serious draw back,

Conventional wisdom holds that slowing population growth is the key to solving a vast array of social, economic, and environmental problems. To be sure, in a world of finite resources, unlimited growth in the number of people requiring food, shelter, and work, not to mention access to natural resources, cannot be sustained, But the increasingly singular focus on demographics simply deflects attention from the fundamental social conditions—poverty, inequity, and the object status of women—of which population growth is not the cause, but the consequence,

In India, as in much of the world, women are last in line for education, job training, credit, and sometimes, even food—

despite the fact that raising the status of women is the most effective way both to reduce birth and to achieve higher standards of health and economic productivity,

In India's tradition-bound society, where child bearing is often the only route to status and security, the majority of women have little to gain from having fewer children. The Government, by contrast, is bent on cutting birthrates in half over the next decade, but has shown little commitment to meeting women's needs.

And so a vicious cycle is perpetuated. As long as the status of women remains low, voluntary family planning efforts will continue to founder, tempting the Government to use pressure to meet its demographic goals.

India will surpass China as the World's most populous country by the middle of the next century, each day the number of people who lack access to adequate food, health care, housing, clean water, and education spirals upward.

FEMALE EDUCATION

Female education is the single most influential determinant of both lower birthrates and increasing empowerment for women,

Indian society manages to devote fewer resources to educating its girls than its boys. At the household level, cultural restrictions on female behaviour combined with the need for cheap household labour create a sharp gender gap in literacy. In both the Hindu and Moslem traditions, for example, notions of female "modesty" and "purity" dictate that unmarried females remain separate from unrelated males. Because the bulk of India's teachers are men, and most schools educate boys and girls under the same roof, many traditional families keep their daughters home, regardless of their income, Moreover, parents are apt to invest in educating girls only when they perceive that long-term gains will outweigh immediate costs.

For the impoverished majority, the expense of sending a girl to school—paying for uniforms, books, and prohibitive, especially when young girls are required to work at home and in the fields,

Women's lack of knowledge translates directly into poor nutrition and health for themselves and their offspring. In turn, these conditions cause high infant mortality—for which many women compensate by having more babies.

NUTRITION AND HEALTH

Nutritional and Health Status is also marked by gender disparity. Both boys and girls in India are nutritionally disadvantaged, as nearly half of the country's households fail to provide even the minimum daily caloric requirements. But malnutrition is far more prevalent among females than males. From birth, male children consistently receive more and better food than their sisters, even though the nutritional needs of prepubescent boys and girls are virtually identical. Boys, given the same level of illness, are taken to doctors more often than girls. As a result of this neglect, far more girls than boys die in the critical period between infancy and age five,

Discrimination in feeding and health care produces one of India's most provocative signs of gender bias: In fact, the ratio of women to men in the country has been declining,

WOMEN AND FAMILY INCOME

Son preference and the subsequently biased allocation of family resources is based on a series of myths the Indian Government has failed to combat. One is the notion—not peculiar to India—that females do not contribute to family income. Throughout the World, Women bear the "invisible" burdens of unpaid domestic work and child-bearing, the economic value of which is rarely reflected by official statistics,

Young girls in India generally work longer hours than boys of the same age. By age 10, girls in low income families are working eight or more hours a day assisting their mothers by tending siblings, collecting water and fire-wood, herding small animals, weeding fields, or facing the daily grind of low-paid child labour in the marketplace.

The poorer the family, the more vital the economic contribution that women and girls make especially in the growing number of female-headed households,

INDIFFERENCE TOWARDS WOMEN

The attempts to enhance agricultural productivity disproportionately benefit men. Expansion of the irrigated area allocated to cash corps, such as groundnut and cotton, has come at the expense of food crops on which women depend to feed their families. And while the mechanization of plowing and levelling that comes with these projects reduces the traditional workload of men, that for women actually increases, women still must carry out by hand the tasks of weeding, turning soil, and harvesting, but over much larger areas.

The result is to deepen women's poverty and enhance the perceived value of having many children to help with chores.

Not surprisingly, the share of married couples of reproductive ago using contraceptives...now 40 per cent—is low, and moat of these are holder couples who turned to sterilization (counted as a form of contraceptive) only after having large families,

This bleak situation is shadowed by an ominous fact of history, Past attempt to reduce births in the absence of social changes enhancing women's status have been accompanied by increases in violence against females—in the beating and abandonment of women who don't bear sons, in female infanticide and child neglect, and in the rising use of abortion for sex-selection.

Experience shows that even in India, with its immense tangle of troubles, well-designed programs can produce dramatic improvements in family health while improving women's status and reducing births.

Increasing young girls' access to education and offering older women a chance for learning are essential to increasing female autonomy. Requisite steps include serious efforts to train and hire more female teachers, to set up literacy and tutoring campaigns in every state, and to encourage the growth of women's empowerment groups to foster changes at the village level. These strategies already have been proven in the southern state of Kerala, internationally lauded for its dramatic gains in the health and economic status of women and in slowing population growth,

Equally important are broad public education campaigns to raise awareness of be immense value of women's work and welfare to families and societies, The mass media also could be enlisted in the effort to change dramatically social perceptions of women's roles by depicting positive Images of women and their economic contribution to society,

Much of the battle to win recognition of the importance of women's lives and health to societies will have to be fought by women themselves. Indications are that women are responding to the challenge.

By filling the existing demand for quality voluntary family planning services, the Government can make cuts in birth-rates of at least 25 per cent over the next decade, thereby starting the process toward reducing the country's population. Equally critical to a long term strategy of sustainable development is a sustained political commitment to improve the status of women throughout India. Only by working toward all these objectives simultaneously can the dreams of women for full partnership in society come true,

9

FIGHTING FOR EQUALITY ON ALL FRONTS

In the wake of unemployment, global competition and deregulation, more and more women are joining an unforgiving job market. Are they in a position to exercise force against—the discrimination they experience, and can they impose equality of opportunity? To change things, women need to enter into combat on several fronts.

"For a long time, companies considered publicity to be a luxury and, in difficult times, the 'advertising and communications' budget was always the first to be slashed. Today, employers have become more aware that publicity has become a trump card in their strategy. Why can't a similar awareness become possible on the subject of women's employment?"

Financial problems and an evolution of mentality are the two core themes discussed in this paper on the Equality or Women in the World of work.

A DUAL OBSERVATION

It is of a two-fold general observation: women are more increasingly joining the ranks of the active population: However, this trend is not matched by a parallel improvement in the quality of jobs to which they have access.

It is foreseen that women's rate of participation will be close to that of men by the year 2000. In developing countries, the rate of women's activity is only 31 per cent on average, but this figure does not take into account the very large female participation in the informal sector and in agriculture. Thus, for example, in India, the adoption of a more general definition of "economic activity" pushed the participation of women from 13 to 88 per cent.

Women remained constrained in a relatively limited number of "feminine" sectors and occupations which are generally less well-paid and are less prestigious. During the last decade, however, an upward trend has emerged and more women are acceding to management and administrative posts and to specialized and technical professions. Moreover, an increasing number of women are setting up their own businesses. It can be noted, nonetheless, that very few salaried women are able to reach the higher echelons of responsibility due to the well-known "glass ceiling".

Among other disturbing observations is the increase in part-time work, which is especially prevalent among women with young children; other types of a typical work include temporary and occasional jobs, home-work and subcontracting. Part-time workers are often young women who are less educated and less qualified than the average, which makes them more vulnerable. In Africa, in Asia and in Latin America, women are being called upon more and more to find work in the informal sector.

Even though, some progress has been made in the area of wages, women's salaries are still between one-half and 80 per cent of those, earned by men. Women's work is under-estimated in most of the societies, and their income does not match their contribution to the economy. The difference in wages cannot be attributed to conditions of work alone. In the United States, in 1994 a woman in her twenties was likely to be earning 90 per cent of the rate of salary of her male counterpart.

FINANCIAL PROBLEMS

Financial problems and mentality issues emerged as two essential factors at every stage of the analysis of the causes of these persistent differences. The Forum's participants' general consensus was that they should be tackled first of all.

Financial implications cannot be separated from the issue of women's employment, whether it is to justify its need or on the contrary to discourage it, or to explain the absence or lack of training of women who are available in the job market. Some examples are:

- In the countries in transition in Central and Eastern Europe companies under-pressure to increase profits do not want to maintain social support services, which earlier had backed women's participation in the active population. These pressures are compelling women to leave the job market as the cost of child care increases.
- In developing countries, especially in Asia, Africa and Latin America, the worsening of poverty and the increase in the number of single-parent families are requiring women to turn towards income-generating activities, but the lack of training and difficult access to credit constitute a major handicap.
- In Thailand, one of the major causes of young village girls resorting to prostitution is the state of poverty of their families, who are unable to afford secondary schooling for then.,

PREJUDICES AND STEREOTYPES

Several examples can also be found in the persisting traditions and stereotypes which are an obstacle in the path of women's march to equality of opportunity in the world of work.

- The Nordic countries, in particular Sweden, have instituted a parental leave which enables either one of the parents to take care of the young children at home; but it can be noted that very few fathers avail themselves of this opportunity.

- The status of a profession falls as the number' of women entering it increases; salary levels thus become relatively less competitive. This trend is particularly clear in the teaching professions and in some medical professions.
- Measures of positive action are becoming more and more general. They cannot be successful unless they tackle discrimination on all fronts, together with the fixed ideas that are prevalent on the subject of the sexes. In fact, solutions to the financial problems that women's work causes are themselves going through an evolution in mentalities.

In a highly competitive job market, opportunities available to women are conditioned by the comparative cost of women's labour, as it is perceived by the employer. By virtue of the legislation in force in the majority of countries, the obligations linked to maternity protection and family responsibilities tend to increase the direct costs of women workers; generally, employers bridge this gap by lowering the wages of women or limiting recruitment to childless women. This form of discrimination can also so as far as requiring medical certificates to guarantee sterility.

A GLOBAL PROGRAMME

To avoid such tendencies, efforts should be channelled toward two fronts. First, evaluating the relationship between a real cost-benefit (including the criterion of effective productivity) with a view toward eliminating the false idea that women workers are more expensive.

Secondly, making sure that in legislation, in practice and especially in the mentality of men and women all around the reproductive function and care of persons are recognized as social functions whose costs should be footed by society as a whole.

Recognizing the universal nature of the problem and the various fronts where one would need to enter into combat, this programme should aim at changing the relationship of power between men and women. For this change to become permanent, it will be necessary to consolidate the ground gained as the process continues.

Remedies should be composed of measures touching upon, among other areas, legislation and its control, access to jobs, to training and to resources, the reconciling of professional activities with family responsibility, outreach measures to groups of underprivileged women, improvement of information and research, the participation of women in decision-making and the mobilization of public opinion.

10

POPULATION GROWTH AND JOBS

Since mid-century, the World's Labour Force has more than doubled from 1.2 billion people to 2.7 billion, outstripping the growth in job creation. As a result, the United Nations International Labour Organization estimates that nearly 1 billion people, approximately 30 per cent of the global work force, are unemployed or underemployed (working but not earning enough to meet basic needs). Over the next half-century, the World will need to create more than 1.9 billion jobs all of them in the developing world just to maintain current levels of employment.

As economists often note, while population growth may boost labour demand (through economic activity and demand for goods), it will most definitely boost labour supply. During the next 50 years, almost 40 million people will enter the global labour force-defined as those between the ages of 15 and 65 seeking work-each year. Between 1995 and 2050, some 1.9 billion additional jobs will need to be created to absorb these new would-be workers. The most pressing needs will be found in the World's poorest nations-a sobering example of the vicious cycle linking poverty and population growth.

As the children of today represent the workers of tomorrow, the interaction between population growth and jobs is most acute in nations with young population. Nations such as Peru, Mexico, Indonesia, and Zambia with more than half their population below the age of 25 will feel the burden of this labour flood. In the Middle East and Africa, 40 per cent of the population is under the age of 15. Since new entrants into the labour force were born at least 15 years ago, measures to reduce population growth have a delayed effect on the growth of the labour force, highlighting the urgency of taking action on population.

Nowhere is the employment challenge greater than in Africa, where at least 40 per cent of the population lives in absolute poverty. Although, 8 million people entered the sub-Saharan work force in 1997, by 2030 this resource-scarce region will have to absorb more than 17 million new entrants each year. Over the next half-century, Nigeria's labour-force is projected to grow by 246 per cent and Ethiopia's will soar by 337 per cent-both faster than growth of the general population. At current growth-rates, the size of the labour-force in sub-Saharan Africa will more than triple by 2050.

As a result of unprecedented population growth and increasing acceptance of female participation in the work force, the number of people seeking jobs in the Middle-East and North Africa, a region already plagued by double-digit unemployment rates, will double in the next 50 years. In Algeria, where unemployment stands at 22 per cent, the labour force is growing at a staggering 4.2 per cent annually, and the number seeking work will more than double by 2050. Egypt alone will need to create 26 million more jobs by 2050 as its total population hits 115 million.

Nations throughout Asia will also see phenomenal increases in the numbers seeking work, including Pakistan, where the work force will grow from 70 million in 1998 to 205 million by 2050. Over the next 25 years, India will add nearly 10 million to its work force each year. During the same period, China will add nearly 6 million annually due to population growth alone, compounding the work shortages caused by the current flood of migrants to China's coastal cities and by massive layoffs-estimated at more than 30 million—as state-run operations are scaled back.

Nations are hard-pressed to educate and train rapidly growing number of young people in marketable skills for the global workplace. Moreover, meeting the basic needs of a growing population draws scarce foreign exchange and other resources from investments in education and job creation. Throughout the world, young people entering the work force are increasingly faced with unemployment and social marginalization. In most societies, unemployment rates for those under 25 are substantially higher than for older people.

Surplus farmland once served as a traditional source of employment for growing populations, as new land could be plowed to generate work and income. However, global per capita Greenland has dropped by half and considerably more in certain nations since 1950. Moreover, the mechanization of agriculture fuels the exodus of job seekers into the world's urban areas, where unemployment is often most acute, heavily reliant on natural capital in the past, future job creation will require massive amounts of financial capital to jump-start the industrial and service sectors.

As the balance between the demand and supply of labour is tipped by population growth, wages—the price of labour-tend to decrease. And in a situation of labour surplus, the quality of jobs may not improve as fast for workers will settle for longer hours, fewer benefits and less control over work activities.

Employment is the key to obtaining food, housing, health services, and education, in addition to providing self-respect and self-fulfilment. Rising numbers of unemployed people could drive global poverty and hunger to precarious levels, fuelling political instability.

11

POPULATION GROWTH AND INCOME

Global economic output, the total of all goods, and services produced, grew from $ 5 trillion in 1950 to $ 29 trillion in 1998, expanding more than twice as fast as population. This increase of nearly six-fold boosted incomes rather substantially for most of humanity. Growth of the world economy from 1990 to 1997 exceeded the growth during the 10,000 years from the beginning of agriculture until 1950.

Economic output per person climbed from just over @ 1,900 in 1950 to nearly @ 5,000 in 1997, a gain of 163 per cent Although, there is an enormous income gap between industrial and developing countries, the latter's economies are growing far more rapidly. Growth in industrial countries has slowed to scarcely 2 per cent a year during the 1990s, compared with nearly 6 per cent a year in developing nations.

The fastest-growing region in the World from 1990 to 1997 was Asia, which averaged nearly 8 per cent annually. This growth was led by China, whose economy has been increasing at nearly 10 per cent a year throughout much of this decade, making it the world's fastest-growing economy. Since 1980, China's economic output has doubled every eight years.

Incomes have risen most rapidly in developing countries where population growth has slowed the most, including, importantly, the countries of East Asia-South Korea, Taiwan, China, Thailand, Indonesia, and Malaysia, Concentrating early on reducing birth-rates helped to boost savings to invest in education, health care, and the infrastructure needed by a modern industrial society.

At the other end of the spectrum, African countries—largely ignoring family planning—have been overwhelmed by the sheer numbers of young people who need to be educated and employed. With population growth-rates remaining at close to 3 per cent or more a year, most of any economic growth that occurred has been absorbed by the increasing population, leaving little to raise incomes.

The enormous growth during the 1990s, particularly in East Asia, is due to the huge increase in private capital flows into developing countries. Between 1990 and 1997, annual private capital flows increased from $ 42 billion to $ 256 billion, a gain of more than sixfold. This substantial amount of money dwarfs traditional flows in public funds under international aid programs.

Although, incomes in much of the developing world are rising rapidly, they are not rising for everyone. The World Bank estimates that 1.3 billion of the World's people subsist on $1 a day or less. For this one fifth of humanity, trapped at a subhuman level of existence, there has not been any meaningful progress.

The sources of growth are changing. In earlier times, most of the growth was in agriculture. Since the advent of the Industrial Revolution, however, more and more of the growth has been concentrated in industry. Then beginning around mid-century, the services sector—insurance, banking, education began to expand rapidly, accounting for most of the change in the industrial world. More recently, growth 'has been concentrated in the information sector as computerization of the economy and telecommunications have grown at extra-ordinary rates.

The good news is that the global economy has been expanding at a near record pace during the 1990s, the bad news is that the economy, as now structured, is outgrowing the

Earth's Ecosystem. The result is excessive pressures on the natural systems and resources. As noted in the first section of this paper, from 1950 to 1997 the use of number more than doubled. That of paper increased sixfold, the fish catch increased nearly five-fold, grain consumption nearly tripled, fossil fuel burning nearly quandrupled, and air and water pollutants multiplied several-fold, the unfortunate reality is that the economy continues to expand, but the ecosystem on which it depends does not, creating an increasingly stressed relationship.

If the economy were to expand only enough to cover population growth until 2050, it would need to grow from the $ 29 trillion of 1997 to $ 47 trillion. This, of course, would merely maintain current incomes, unacceptable though, they are for much of humanity. If, on the other hand, the economy were to continue to expand at 3 per cent per year, global economic output would reach $ 138 trillion in the year 2050.

Even the first, more modest, growth projection would likely lead to a deterioration of the Earth's Natural Systems to the point where the economy itself would begin to decline. It is easy to foresee a scenario of continuing forest destruction, aquifer depletion, and ecosystem collapse that would lead to economic decline. If the World cannot simultaneously convert the economy to one that is environmentally sustainable—one that does not destroy its own support systems and move to a lower population trajectory, economic decline will be hard to avoid.

12

ACTION FOR SAFE MOTHERHOOD

Countries vary enormously in terms of the situations and challenges they face and their capacity to address these. However, experience from around the world over the past decade has demonstrated that a number of features are common to successful efforts to address maternal mortality. Reducing maternal mortality requires coordinated, long-term efforts. Actions are needed within families and communities, in society as a whole, in health systems, and at the level of national legislation and policy. Further, interactions among the interventions in these areas are critical to reducing maternal mortality and to building and supporting momentum for change.

LEGISLATIVE AND POLICY ACTIONS

Changes in legislation and policy are essential to ensure safe motherhood. Long-term political commitment is an essential prerequisite. When decision-makers at the highest levels are resolved to address maternal mortality, the resources needed will be mobilized and the essential policy decisions will be taken. Without this level of commitment over the long-term, projects cannot become programmes and activities cannot be sustained.

A supportive social, economic, and legislative environment allows women to overcome the various obstacles that limit their access to health care, such as distance from their homes to appropriate health facilities, lack of transport and, more critically, financial and social barriers. Proper maternal health care is limited when women have to pay for services and essential drugs, and when they must bear substantial hidden costs such as time lost for housework, paid employment, food production, and child care. Legislation that supports women's access to care must be formulated to permit health workers at the periphery of the health system to perform specific life-saving functions. Failing this, only highly skilled health professionals, based largely in urban centres, can provide such care, and only women with sufficient money and the means to reach such centres can benefit from it,

With these objectives, careful review of national laws and policies is necessary, particularly in the following areas:

- **Family Planning:** Statutes that restrict women's access to family planning services (*e.g.*, by requiring that a woman be married or that she should have her husband's approval) should be repealed. Policies must ensure that all couples and individuals have access to good-quality, voluntary, client-oriented, and confidential family planning information and to services that offer a wide choice of effective contraceptive methods. Policies should address regulatory, social, economic, and cultural factors that limit women's control over sexuality and reproduction, in order that pregnancies that are too early, too late, or too frequent may be avoided.
- **Adolescents and Children:** Policies and programmes should encourage later marriage and child-bearing and an expansion of the economic and educational opportunities for girls and women. Promotion of good nutrition in childhood and adolescence, as well as supplementation if necessary during pregnancy, provides protection for both women and their future children. Policies should also enable adolescents to take responsibility for and protect their sexual and

reproductive health, and facilitate their access to health information and services. All children, before they reach the age at which they become sexually active, need to be taught the risks of unprotected sex and helped to develop the skills needed to protect themselves from sexual coercion.

- **Barriers to Access:** Assigning health workers trained in mid-wifery to village-based health facilities can help overcome problems of distance and transport. Health workers should also be trained to deal sympathetically with women patients. Policies should support the provision of services at minimum cost; at the same time, health workers should have job security, be paid adequate wages, and be provided with sufficient supplies to do their jobs. Policies that will increase women's decision-making power, particularly in regard to their own health, are also essential.

- **Regulation of Practice:** Protocols and statutes aimed at providing both routine maternal care and referral facilities for obstetric complications at each level of the health system need to be developed. Responsibilities at each level for supervision, deployment of health care personnel, remuneration, and reporting procedures must be defined nationally. Development and promotion of education and training curricula are important, as is the setting of national norms and standards to govern the selection of trainees, trainers, and supervisors.

- **Delegation of Authority:** Services should be decentralized so that facilities are available as close to people's homes as possible. Adequate supplies and equipment and trained staff should be available in all health facilities, particularly in rural and remote areas, together with written policies and protocols to guide service provision and to allow certain functions to be delegated to personnel at lower levels (when appropriately trained).

- **Abortion:** Availability of services for management of abortion complications and post-abortion care should be ensured by appropriate legislation. Where abortion is not prohibited by law, facilities for the safe termination of pregnancy should be made available. National policy can discourage unsafe abortion practices by promoting protection against unwanted pregnancy, and national health campaigns to publicize the risks of unsafe abortion and the need to recognize and seek treatment for abortion complications.

13

SAFE MOTHERHOOD IS A HUMAN RIGHTS ISSUE

The death of a woman during pregnancy or child-birth is not only a health issue but also a matter of social injustice. Of the human rights currently acknowledged in national constitutions and in regional and international human rights treaties, many can be applied to safe motherhood. Many such treaties and conventions are based on the 1948 Declaration of Human Rights (1), they include the Convention on the Elimination of All Forms of Discrimination against Women; (2), the Convention on the Rights of the Child (3), the European Convention for the Protection of Human Rights and Fundamental Freedom (4), the American Convention on Human Rights (5), and the African Charter on Human and Peoples' Rights (6).

Human rights of relevance to safe motherhood can be grouped into the following four principal categories:

- *Rights Relating to Life, Liberty and Security of the Person*: Which require Governments to ensure both access to appropriate health care during pregnancy and childbirth, and women's rights to decide whether, when, and how often to bear children. Governments must therefore, address factors within the economic, legal, social, and health systems that deny women these fundamental rights.

- *Rights Relating to the Foundation of Families and of Family Life*: Which require Governments to provide access to health-services and other facilities that women need to establish families and to enjoy life within a family.

- *Rights Telating to Health Care and the Benefits of Scientific Progress, Including Health Information and Education*: Which require Governments to provide access to good sexual and reproductive health care with appropriate referral systems. The measures needed to ensure safe motherhood can be provided through primary health care irrespective of a country's level of Economic Development. Central to these rights is information on a range of reproductive health issues, including family-planning, abortion, and sex education.

- *Rights Relating to Equality and Nondiscrimination*: Which require Governments to provide access to services such as education and health care without discriminatory grounds such as sex, marital status, age, and socioeconomic class. Discriminatory policies include requirements for a woman to obtain the consent of her husband for particular health care interventions, requirements for parental authorization which have a differential impact on girls, and laws that criminalize medical procedures that only women need. Governments are in violation of their obligations when they fail to implement laws that effectively protect women's interests or to allocate health resources to meet women's particular need for safe pregnancy and child-birth.

The actions that Governments need to take to promote safe motherhood as a human right fall into three groups:

- *Reform of Laws* that prevent women from attaining the highest possible levels of health and nutrition needed for safe pregnancy and childbirth and that inhibit access to reproductive health information and services such as laws requiring women in need of health care to seek the authorization of husbands or other family members first.

- *Implemention of Laws* that foster women's rights to good health and nutrition and that protect women's health interests such as laws that prohibit child marriage, female genital mutilation, rape, and sexual abuse. Every effort should be made to implement laws that encourage the healthy timing of births, such as those that support the education of girls, set a minimum age for marriage, and ensure women's access to essential health care.
- *Application of Human Rights* in national legislation and policy to advance safe motherhood.

14

WHAT IS KNOWN ABOUT REDUCING MATERNAL MORTALITY?

Historical records demonstrate the significant improvements that can be achieved when key interventions are In place. Reductions in maternal mortality took place in Sweden during the 1800s, for example, as a result of a national policy favouring professional midwifery care for all births, coupled with establishment of standards for quality of care. By the beginning of the 20th century, maternal mortality in Sweden was the lowest around 230 per 1,00,000 live births compared with over 500 per 1,00,000 in the mid-1880s. In Denmark, Japan, Netherlands, and Norway, similar strategies produced comparable results. In England and Wales, significant reductions in maternal mortality were not apparent until the 1930s; at the national level, political commitment to the strategy was achieved only slowly and the introduction of professional midwifery was correspondingly delayed. In every case, however, the key to these improvements was the institution of fully professional maternity care.

In the USA, where strategy focused on hospital delivery by doctors, maternal mortality remained high because it proved difficult to establish adequate regulatory frameworks and mechanisms to ensure quality of care. In 1930, the maternal mortality ratio in the USA was still 700 per 1,00,000 live births compared with 430 in England and Wales.

More recently, India witnessed significant reductions in maternal mortality in a relatively short period. From a level of over 1500 per 1,00,000 live births in 1940-1945, maternal mortality fell to 555 per 1,00,000 in 1950-1955, 239 per 1,00,000 within 10 years, and 95 per 1,00,000 by 1980. The figure is now 30 per 1,00,000. These improvements followed the introduction of a system of health facilities around the country allied to an expansion of midwifery skills and the spread of family planning. During the 1950s most births in India took place at home with the assistance of untrained birth attendants. By the end of the 1980s over 85 per cent of all births were attended by trained personnel.

Similar evidence of the effectiveness of health care interventions is available from China, Cuba, and Malaysia. These countries established community-based maternal health care systems comprising prenatal, delivery, and postpartum care and a system of referral to a higher level of care in the event of obstetric complications.

What these examples clearly demonstrate is that a country's overall economic wealth is not in itself the most important determinant of maternal mortality. There are numerous other examples of countries with modest levels of GNP which have achieved low maternal mortality.

15

ONE BATTLE AFTER ANOTHER

Women fought for their rights throughout the twentieth-century. In the past several decades, their struggle has truly become global, but all is far from won. We often hear that this will be century of women, in light of the tremendous strides that have been made in the past thirty years or so. Although, it is far too soon to confirm this prediction, it can safely be asserted that the twentieth century was marked by their struggle to leave the home, where they were confined by the ancestral division of roles along gender lines. Around the world, women have campaigned to win the rights they have been denied and to build, side-by-side with men, the future of the planet.

True, such struggles had already been waged in the past, although, they were deliberately shunned in official historical accounts. But the brief revolts of this special "minority", which accounts for over half of humanity, did not change the place of women in their societies. They may have ruled the roost, sometimes enjoying undeniable respect, but nevertheless they were still born to serve men and bring their husbands' descendants into the world.

EDUCATION: THEIR FIRST STRUGGLE

Yet, at the start of the twentieth-century, the traditional distribution of roles, seemingly legitimised by every religion and frozen in a "natural" order., began to crumble under the two-pronged assault of modernisation and women's struggle for their collective emancipation. They waged many battles to gradually obtain, despite set-backs, a change in their status—which is still far from achieved.

The first struggle of the twentieth-century was for education. In 1861, a young woman graduated in Finance with a baccalaureate, a high school leaving examination, for the first time. In 1900, the first female university was founded in Japan. The same year, girls won the right to secondary education in Egypt and the first girls' school opened in Tunisia. Young women who could made the most of these new educational opportunities, not only to become better household managers and good educators for their children, as the main discourse of the period suggests, but also to do something unprecedented: to enter the forbidden spheres of public life, to exercise citizenship and to participate in politics. Throughout the twentieth-century, women waged a battle on two fronts: by fighting for their own rights and taking part in the major social political emancipation movements.

The earliest feminist movements, which first appeared in the West in the late nineteenth century, focused on workplace and civil rights issues. Industry needed women's labour, which was underpaid in comparison with that of their male counterparts. 'Equal pay for equal work!' demanded American and European women, who began setting up their own trade unions and organizing strikes. They made unquestionable strides, but after more than one century of struggle, most women around the world still earn less pay for equal work.

THE RIGHT TO VOTE

The second objective of the twentieth-century's pioneers was participation in public life, which hinged first and foremost on having the right to vote. The struggle was long and sometimes violent, as shown by the British "suffragettes" who demonstrated in the streets or Chinese women who made their demands heard by invading their Country's New Parliament in 1912.

Everywhere, the fierce resistance of the political world progressively yielded to determined women's movements.

CONTROL OVER THEIR OWN BODIES

For a while, women's rights movements took a back seat to the Second World War and liberation struggles in the European Colonies. The fight against fascism and, after 1945, colonialism, mobilized all their energy. Women distinguished themselves in these struggles, but that did not suffice to establish their rights as a gender. However, the world continued to change. With independence, many women in the South won access to schooling, salaried employment and, in a few exceptional cases, the closed world of politics. In Western countries, the post-war period saw them enter the work force on a massive scale. The gap between social reality and the discriminatory laws defended by exclusively male power structures grew wider.

In the West, the second generation of feminists emerged in the wake of the libertarian movements of 1968. Picking up where their elders left off, they broadened the scope of their demands, for late—twentieth-century feminists no longer aspired to the right to be "just like men". Challenging the claim of the "white male" to represent university, their goal was to achieve equality while remaining distinct as women. The women's liberation movement that first emerged in the American middle-class claimed the right to control one's own body. Feminists fought for contraception and abortion rights in many countries where one or both were against the law, and for autonomy and equality within the couple. "The personal is political", proclaimed women inspired by Marxism and psychoanalysis. "Workers of the world, who washes your socks?" chanted demonstrators in the streets of Paris in the 1970s. In France, the Veil Law legalizing abortion unleashed emotional debate in 1974.

Many Third World women could not identify with the struggles being waged in the West and insisted on leading their own battles at their own pace. However, these Western feminist movements breathed new life into the cause. Recognizing the changes and proclaiming their intention to accelerate them, the United Nations declared 1975 "International Women's Year" and organized the first international women's conference in Mexico City.

Already proclaimed in the Universal Declaration of Human Rights in 1948, sexual equality was reasserted in 1929 by the Convention on the Abolition of All Forms of Discrimination Against Women, which became a precious emancipation tool in the North as well as the South. At UN conferences in Copenhagen in 1980, Nairobi in 1985 and Beijing in 1995, women from both hemispheres found common ground, demanding the right to "have a child if I want it, when I want it," rejecting Malthusian principles and claiming their place in political bodies that until then had decided the World's future without them, struggling against religious fundamentalism that jeopardizes their modest gains.

MISOGYNY OF THE POLITICAL CLASS

Of course, the struggle of Kuwaiti women against those who have denied that the right to vote or Indian women against the forced abortion of female foetuses is not the same as American women's battle against their own fundamentalists or French women's campaign against the misogyny take different approaches depending on the continent and do not necessarily have the same priorities, but the struggle has nonetheless become global during the past several decades. In the last twenty-five years, women have gradually increased their presence in public life, although it can hardly be said that the doors are wide open for them. From Africa to Asia, women's organizations have multiplied and acquired experience.

But their victories remain incomplete and the future is uncertain. From the nightmare of Afghan women to the ways in which equality is resisted in the so-called most advanced countries, the obstacles show that there is still a long way to go. Will women see the end of the struggle in this century that has just begun, the one which supposedly belongs to them?

16

FOR A FAIR SHARING OF TIME

Women may have entered public life on a massive scale, but they are still on their own when it comes to running the household. A new balance must be struck if there is to be genuine democracy. At the drawn of the 21st century, states and the international community can no longer refute the fact that humanity is made up of two sexes, not just one. This discovery, a precious legacy of the century that just closed, has brought women's existence into the limelight. One of the great democratic challenges for societies over the next century will be to mature so that both sexes are able to live their lives on an equal footing, with all their differences, contrasting history and culture, but also with equal rights and responsibilities.

Women's rise to power and their participation in politics are the vital signs of a healthy democracy. If only this vision that emerged from the 1995 Beijing Women's Conference could spread worldwide! One can call it a radicalisation of democracy. When women take part in the public arena, contributing to the ongoing, shared effort to shape better ways of living together, a qualitative leap occurs. Their participation fills a gap which has until now prevented the emergence of a truly Democratic Culture.

ARCHAIC ATTITUDES

But attitudes are not the only obstacle to women's ambitions. The structure of society and the way men and women run their daily lives are other stumbling blocks. The Inter-American Development Bank has had the good idea of giving the Institute for Cultural Action, and NGO in Rio de Janeiro, the task of setting up a pilot programme to train women for positions of political and social power. Participants include trade union and NGO leaders, key figures from the black and indigenous communities, company executives, civil servants and policy-makers.

These women of different ages, educational backgrounds and ethnic origins are all aware of one fact: they are paying a very high price for a social contract that was negotiated when women were in a position of weakness, and agree that this has to change.

RE-MAPPING THE DIVISION BETWEEN PUBLIC AND PRIVATE LIFE

In *Rio de Janeiro* revealed that there is an urgent need to re-organize the use of time, to strike a new balance between responsibilities and to re-map the division between public and private life. Household tasks must be recognised as time consuming, socially and economically vital and a serious check on women's ambitions.

Women in positions of power must constantly prove that they can behave like men. They keep quiet about having to look after children, run a household and care for elderly parents. Bringing those issues out into the open would mean admitting "flaws" that men do not have, for the simple reason that they delegate such work to their wives.

By drawing a veil of silence over their home life as if it were something illicit, women are allowing a basic fact to be hidden: the world of work relies on a domestic zone run by them. Women have changed, but the world of work has not and they are reaching the point of exhaustion. Filled with a deep sense of injustice, they are asking themselves: "Where did I go wrong?" understanding that humanity is composed of two different but equal sexes has several implications. Society must redefine itself because women are turning up in public carrying children in their arms and breast-feeding them, and because they have their own awareness and language that come from life experiences which are different from those of men.

AN UNTENABLE DOUBLE BURDEN

Articulating issues affecting public and private life is complicated, but that does not mean the equation is impossible of that the problems they raise should be brushed aside especially since the Two-Worlds of public and private life are intertwined and mutually supportive. The balance between the two has now been upset. Women have entered public life on a massive scale, but the organization of home life how time is used and who is responsible for what tasks is still the same, as if nothing had changed. And yet such a world, where women are expected to soldier on just as before, "simply" adding to their lives experiences hitherto reserved to men, is called egalitarian.

That misunderstanding is fueled by and age-old tradition of dismissing the world of women, even by women themselves. Because society does not consider what they do in the home as having any major social significance, it fails to add this part of their lives to the other side of the equation.

This is why the massive migration of women from the home to the public arena is occurring without societies having to think seriously about how and by whom domestic work will be done in the future (and which women still do, but at what cost!). The double burden, resulting from an out dated social contract, is putting women under mounting pressure by speeding up their lives to an untenable pace. We are facing a social problem that society as a whole must solve and not, as many think, a problem that women must settle by working even harder.

As new areas of power open up to women, both sexes must take a fresh look at how they use time. Rearranging it is a challenge to society's imagination. But has this necessity sunk into the minds of decision-makers? I do not think so. This poses a major problem because it is a missing building block in the construction of our democracies.

The everyday work is proof of this. Women must put these issues on the political and economic agenda, thereby contributing to a more radical definition of democracy. Feminism's new demand for a different sharing of time also opens a debate that goes beyond the interests of women alone. In the final analysis, time and its constants define the limits of our own lives and the range of choices we make, in accordance with the meaning we give to our own existence.

The equality equation is increasingly complex. It is not enough to wipe out the last traces of discrimination in public life. A new definition of equality will emerge when both sexes start sharing responsibility in the private realm. Otherwise, the issue will be distorted and women will lose all chance of succeeding in public life.

17

NO PROGRESS WITHOUT A SECULAR SOCIETY

Every day, women continue to be victims of rape, trafficking, acid-throwing, dowry deaths and other kinds of torture. At the opening of this new-century, women are still not considered as equal human-beings in many parts of the world, Religion and patriarchy continue to have an all-encroaching hold on their lives, maintaining and justifying their age-old oppression. In some South Asian Societies, this hold is even increasing.

I do not believe that there can be real equality in a society dominated by religion. Western countries speak repeatedly about the necessity of economic development to alleviate poverty. But, this is not enough. Some oil rich Countries may be economically developed, but women are deprived of all rights. The supremacy of religion is incompatible with freedom of expression, Women's Rights and Democracy. This is why I see religion as the main enemy of women's development.

We have to act on several fronts at once. First of all, improving access to education. In a society like Bangladesh, 80 per cent of women are illiterate. For centuries women have been taught they are the slaves of men. It is very hard to change their minds, to make them aware of their oppression, to give them a sense of their independence. This educational effort has to go hand in hand with a secular feminist movement in society. Such movements have to start within the country and they cannot take hold when people are uneducated and unaware of their oppression. I'm not sure you can accomplish much from the outside, except to expose in the media the atrocities women in all too many countries face in their day to day lives.

In some countries, this movement is emerging, but very timidly, and it has a slim margin of maneuver. It has the uphill task of fighting for the repeal of religious laws and the introduction of a uniform civil code. So far, it tends to be constituted by a few individual feminists who are forced to be diplomatic, to compromise with fundamentalists, be they men or women. But they are trying to change the system, step by step, and it will take a very long-time. People are not yet ready to do away with religious laws that impact upon every aspect of society, from education and health to the workplace and the home.

For women's status to change, we also need enlightened leaders who believe in equality. In countries of South Asia women with a strong voice do not have the support of political leaders, whether they be men or women. Look at the countries in which women are in politics, or even heads of state. Does it follow that women in those countries are emancipated? Because of long-standing vested interests, such leaders continue to back measures that oppress women. They are not ideologically committed to changing these conditions. In South Asia, most of the women who become heads of state are religious, and like men, they adhere to the religious objectives of the Establishment. Until a society is not based on religion and women and considered equal to men before the law, I do not think that politics will advance the cause of women.

Until a society is not based on religion and women are considered equal to men before the law, I do not think that politics will advance the cause of women. In Western countries, women are educated, they are treated equally, they have access to jobs. In these conditions, their participation in politics has a meaning.

Education, a secular feminist movement, and leaders—both men and women—committed to equality and justice. This is what it will take to change the dire conditions which too many women still face today. It will take a very long time, but we are here to work towards that end.

18

TAKING A LEAD IN THE FIGHT AGAINST POVERTY

(World Bank and IMF Speed Implementation of Their New Strategy)

A change in development policy strategy in the poorest countries is at present being prepared with incredible speed. The IMF-style structural adjustment programmes that have been criticised for many years are being scrapped. The countries are now to take their own-decisions on their paths to development. Their Governments will no longer formulate poverty reduction programmes top-down, but in an intensive and long-term dialogue with societal groups and organisations. Governments and institutions of the North commit themselves to supporting these processes, such as by debt relief on an unprecedented scale. Dream or reality?

NEW STRATEGY PAPER

Behind this euphoria lines a new abbreviation, PRSP, standing for Poverty Reduction Strategy Paper, which the IMF and World Bank invented last year. The G-7 Countries in Cologne not only announced debt relief for the Heavily Indebted Poor Countries (HIPCs) but also demanded that it must serve above all for poverty reduction. The PRSP concept was then presented at the annual conference of the two Bretton Woods Organisations

The most important principles of the new "super weapon" in the fight against poverty are:

- PRSPs are papers, which describe the medium-term development paths of the poorest countries of the South, particularly their strategies to combat poverty, and by this means enlist international support. A PRSP is not only the prerequisite for granting debt forgiveness in the context of the HIPC initiative. It is also necessary for all new IMF and World Bank loans to the so-called IDA countries, the some 70 poorest countries that receive concessional loans from the World Bank's International Development Agency (IDA). According to the World Bank, PRSPs should also be required for all future pledges of bilateral development assistance.
- Not only social sector programmes, but also the economic and financial policies of the Developing Countries are in future to be aimed at fighting poverty. Previously, the IMF always pronounced that a growth-oriented national economy and a far-reaching integration in the world market would have a trickle-down effect and also benefit the poor. Now the poor are to be asked what policies can help materially to improve their situation.
- PRSPs are to be developed on the basis of self-responsible country ownership. Accordingly, development and structural adjustment strategies are no longer to be developed by the Washington finance institutions, but the countries themselves.
- The heading "country ownership" is to underline that not only Governments are called upon, PRSPs should come into being in a participatory process. That means involvement of trade unions, NGOs, cooperatives, associations, grass roots, groups, political parties and parliaments. A country's PRSP should be developed in a societal debate, a dialogue between Governments on one side and parliamentary, private sector and civil society on the other.

RHETORIC OR REALITY

Are PRSPs the expression of a change of paradigm? In brief, if all what the papers contain is implemented in a consistent and wide-ranging, way, the chances of achieving it are good but there are a number of open questions. The answers to them will have a bearing on success or failure.

- Is the IMF really changing its policy on the poorest countries or merely wrapping its old policy in new words? The growing criticism of the IMF in recent years strengthened latterly by the evaluation of the ESAF (Enhanced Structural Adjustment Facility) programmes, which once again proved their blatant weaknesses called for reaction and is now triggering changes—real or only rhetorical? There will be no more old-style ESAF loans based on macroeconomic structural adjustment programmes. But the credit line remains, and is now called the Poverty Reduction and Growth Facility (PRGF). This will be granted on the basis of the PRSPs, which in each case must also be accepted by the IMF board of directors. How much influence will the IMF have on the design of the PRSPS ? What happens if a Government choose macroeconomic strategies combat poverty which go against previous IMF policy? Open questions. Moreover, there is still no answer to the question of why the IMF is at all coming on with long-term and low-interest lines of credit in the poorest countries.

MIXED FEELINGS WITH REGARD TO WORLD BANK ROLE

- Will the World Bank use the PRSP process to expand its own institutional power further? NGOs in the North and South are viewing this with mixed feelings. Many welcome the fact that for the moment the World Bank appears to be asserting itself against its twin, the IMF. On the other hand, 50 years of experience with World Bank strategies have certainly not strengthened their trust in the Bank's ability to make a convincing fight against poverty. That is why the EURODAD network also questions the role of the World Bank (and the IMF) in the PRSP process. It says the papers should not be presented to the two financial institutions, whose power over the development strategies of countries of the South thus, would increase further. Rather, PRSPs should for example, be laid before a Round Table of all donors chaired by the United Nations Development Programme (UNDP).

OWNERSHIP

- The principles of developing countries being responsible for their own development strategies are as old as it is—in theory—right. There have been frequent complaints about shortcomings in ownership. But now, after decades of development strategies being set and structural adjustment programmes being dictated from outside, the Governments of the poorest countries, which in many cases have only weak institutional capacities, can hardly taken on sole responsibility overnight. In addition, of course, not a few of the countries are ruled by corrupt political elites (promoted from outside over decades) that give little reason to hope they would immediately switch to poverty reduction politics. Scepticism and critical observation is justified even if there is no alternative to Governments of the South taking over greater responsibility.
- Civil society actors are now asked to help out in particular in those countries whose Governments appear to be less trustworthy. A nice idea that has little to do with real life. Civil society actors in developing countries in general and in the poorest countries in particular are extraordinarily weak institutions which in many cases are totally dependent on financing from the North.

The civil society landscape in other countries is even weaker. However, social actors in many countries could make useful contributions to developing sustainable strategies. But that calls for meaningful and lasting support, including financial support, capacity—building, and in some countries also political pressure to gain scope for societal engagement.

It is reasonable that not only the World Bank and other official donors but also, and above all, the northern NGO partners of these actors are now giving much thought to how civil societies in the south can be strengthened.

PARTICIPATION

Even assuming there were civil society actors capable of dialogue, that does not clarify what participation in the PRSP process is really supposed to mean. Is civil society only to be listened to, or can it if necessary refuse to approve a PRSP? What impact would a refusal have on acceptance of the document by the IMF and World Bank and other donor? And in view of the great time pressure, will civil society be at all able to formulate discuss and feed their positions into the process? It could be of decisive importance for the current debate on the PRSP model to delink the urgently needed debt relief from drawing up a PRSP programme, which simply needs more time. For example, it is conceivable that there would be no great problems in granting a country a moratorium on debt servicing so long as a PRSP process is continuing and then for giving debt when it is completed. That would ease the time problem for NGOs and at the same time maintain pressure on Governments actually to arrive at poverty reduction strategies that were developed in a participatory process.

OTHER CAUSES OF POVERTY IN DEVELOPING COUNTRIES

The entire current process is focused on the countries of the South, their Governments and societies. That diverts attention from the responsibility of the donors and creditors. Not only that the IMF's structural adjustment programmes to date have been counterproductive for fighting poverty (why does the IMF not admit that openly just for once?). Not only that the now promised debt reliefs are coming much too late (the debt crisis of the poorest countries was deplored decades ago!). The present strategy also ignores various other exogenous causes of poverty in the South. What impacts do the finance and trade policies of northern countries have on the modest attempts to enable sustainable development in the South? What consequences will the continuing cutting of development budgets have on the South (no one anyway ventures to talk nowadays about the old 0.7 per cent ODA-GNP ratio)? Fort the donors and creditors to now pass the buck of sole responsibility to the Governments of the South and present themselves in the background as noble do-gooders may be a successful strategy in terms of domestic politics, but not an acceptable one for Development Policy.

19

MEASURING POPULATION'S IMPACT

There is no easy way to measure the overall impact of human activities on the environment. Nevertheless, several approaches have been developed as follows :

ENVIRONMENTAL RESOURCE ACCOUNTING

Environmental resource accounting attempts to place an economic value on "environmental goods and services" used - natural resources that conventionally have been regarded as free and used in common . These include unpolluted freshwater clean air, ocean life, forests, and wetlands.

Some economists argue that the value of environmental goods and services should be incorporated into estimates of gross manufactured capital, which depreciates in value overtime, environmental capital (such as forests, fisheries, and unpolluted air and water) currently is not considered to depreciate, and no charge is made against current income as it is used. A country could exhaust its mineral resources, cut down its forests, erode its soils, pollute its acquires, and hunt its wildlife and fisheries to extinction, but measured income would not be affected as these natural assets disappeared.

If natural resources were valued in the same way that manufactured assets are valued, it might help economies learn to use them more efficiently and to conserve them in order to assure continued use in the future. Such valuations also might help indicate the economic benefits of protecting the environment, as well as the ecological benefits. In other terms, instead of continuing to draw down their "environmental capital" until it is gone, economies could begin to live on its interest, maintaining the capital for use indefinitely in the future.

I = P × A × T

The equation I = P × A × T represents another effort to describe the overall impact of humanity on the environment. In the equation :

- I is environmental impact,
- P is population (including size, growth, and distribution),
- A is the level of affluence (consumption per capita), and
- T is the level of technology.

Despite its limitations—for instance, inability to assign actual values to each component or to depict changes in the factors over time—the equation is valuable. In particular, it emphasizes that Developing Countries with large and rapidly growing populations affect the environment, even though their levels of affluence may be low, while at the same time countries in the developed world with little or no population growth have a substantial environmental impact because consumption per capital is so high.

The equation makes clear that slowing population growth is a key part of any strategy to reduce humanity's impact on the environment. For example, even if per capita resource consumption (A) declined or technologies (T) improved enough to reduce the environmental impact (I) of humanity by 10 per cent, this gain would be wiped out in less than a decade because World Population (P) is growing at over 1 per cent per year since per capital consumption of resources is expected to increase as living standards rise, protecting the environment requires more efficient production technologies, less waste, and ultimately a stable world population size.

ECOLOGICAL FOOTPRINTS OF NATIONS

Everybody has an impact on the earth, because they consume the products and services of nature. Their ecological impact corresponds to the amount of nature they occupy to keep them going. In other words, we calculate the 'ecological footprints' of these countries.

CARRYING CAPACITY

The term "carrying capacity" refers to the number of people the earth can support. Logically, population growth must stop at some point, or the earth would become overcrowded and its resources eventually would be depleted. But what is this maximum human population?

This question has been debated since 1798, When English Economists Thomas Malhus predicted that population growth inevitably would outstrip the food ad water supply at some point. Since the estimates of carrying capacity have varied a great deal depending on what assumptions are made out technology, consumption levels, and other factors that are not easily forecast. Some have even argued that the earth's carrying capacity may already have been exceeded in sense that the world consumed at the rate that Americans and Western European·consume.

While nobody can know how many people the earth could support, few would want to find out the hard way — by reaching this theoretical limit. Calculate the maximum number of people who could exist on earth seems less important than determining how resources can be used wisely and managed sustainably to improve living standard without eventually destroying the natural environment that supports life itself.

20

CAN ECONOMIC GROWTH REDUCE POVERTY?

(New Findings on Inequality, Economic Growth and Poverty)

Many people still think first of 'Economic Growth' in relation to poverty reduction. Indeed, their correlation is one of the most-discussed issues of combating poverty. The relationship is of great importance because if there is a clear causal dependency, reducing poverty could fundamentally be limited to measures to promote growth. However, if there was low growth or stagnation it would not be possible to reduce poverty decisively. In the opposite case, that of the phenomena having no causal-relation, promising measures to reduce poverty could be taken up even without economic growth.

Hardly, anyone now explicitly expresses the view that economic development trickles down automatically to the poor. Practical experience has refuted this assumption dating from the early days of development policy in the 1960s. However, a number of studies show Development of Growth and a decline in poverty running parallel. On the other hand, there are also examples which show that despite high economic growth, poverty is not reduced markedly. The common answer to the question this raises is thus: Yes, growth can reduce poverty, but only if additional measures oriented on the poor are taken up. This is often termed pro-poor-growth. But what that means in detail, and whether economic growth as such plays a causal role at all, is not clarified. It is worth taking a look at the arguments on the basis of more recent empirical and theoretical knowledge.

NO DIRECT CAUSALITY BETWEEN GROWTH AND POVERTY REDUCTION

Among the many indicators of poverty, the income of the poor (income poverty) has the closest relationship to economic growth. An increase in gross domestic product and thus national income could, if other factors come into play be linked with an increase in the per capita income of the poor. Such a relationship between economic growth and the income of the poor, however, cannot be described as causal, as is asserted implicitly time and again by the statement that growth is a necessary but not sufficient precondition for poverty reduction. In so far as growth and poverty reduction arise at the same time at the end of a process, they exist alongside each other. It would be almost a tautology to say that the former is the cause or part-cause of the latter. Both express the same thing, namely a change in per capita income as well, and both have similar causes. What matters is recognising what these causes are and what specific factors must come into play so that the income of the poor grows too. Growth as a "prerequisite" or "condition" is then no longer the focus; the priority is asking for specific policies that result in higher incomes for the poor. The detour in thinking about growth is not necessary. Since, however, it is based on similar factors, such as fiscal policy/budget structure, employment policy, combating inflation, and institutional development, economic-growth can also emerge if poverty is reduced. The difference of views lies in the fact that under the heading 'poverty reduction' the aim is no longer growth, but a purposeful reduction of poverty.

Therefore, in reverse, successful combating of poverty can be seen as being the cause of growth insofar as activating the capabilities of the poor and using their productive capacity of the poor and using their productive capacity triggers economic drive.

INDIRECT CAUSALITY BETWEEN GROWTH AND POVERTY REDUCTION?

So even if economic growth fundamentally has no direct causal impact on poverty, growth still can reduce it indirectly. This is the case when due to positive economic development a Government has greater revenue and uses the surplus for combating poverty, for example, by providing such public goods as education and health services. Also in these cases, however, growth is not a compelling precondition. Even without growth greater Government revenue can be achieved for example, by more efficient tax collection. And leeway for social welfare spending can be gained by redistributing the budget, such as by cutting military appropriations. Furthermore, an automatic process is not given because the Government can also use surplus funds for non-social purposes.

Creation of jobs due to increased economic activity can be another indirect link between economic growth and income poverty, if such a development generates income and reduces poverty. But also in this case I see no compelling causality because, for instance, industrial jobs are not necessarily open to the really poor. In addition, these positive impacts occur to a considerable extent only in the event of labour-intensive development. In many countries, however, economic growth is achieved by capital-intensive production.

INEQUALITY, GROWTH AND INCOME POVERTY

If national incomes, grow, a naive observer might assume that the income of the poor must also grow along with it. But that would be a statistical fallacy. Even if only the income of the rich grows, this results in macroeconomic statistics showing a higher per capita income. What the true conditions are is shown as soon as one divides the population statistically into income groups, such as in fifths, as is usual. It then turns out that the bald figures on average per capital growth can certainly cloak a situation where the income of the richest fifth of the population is growing fast while that of the poorest fifth is stagnating. Despite growth, the gap between the two becomes even wider.

The unequal distribution of income (and of other assets such as property and access to social services), and its connection to poverty reduction and growth has recently returned to the forefront of the debate.

It is obvious that inequality and its changes have direct effects on the poverty situation. Does inequality also have an impact on poverty via its relation to growth, because growth promotes or reduces inequality? Earlier, the predominant view was that rapid growth was linked with atleast a temporary increase in inequality, so that a distinct policy of growth initially disadvantaged the poor.

The current dominant view is that growth has no foreseeable effects on inequality and that inequality changes only very slowly, in reverse, however, it is assumed that greater equality is a determinant of growth. According to that view, an indirect relationship between poverty on one side and inequality as a factor dependent upon growth on the other is not given.

That leads to the conclusion that fair distribution has more weight than growth. Fair distribution, however, does not depend upon growth. An appropriate policy is possible at any time, not only after an economic situation has improved. The notion that still shimmers through the debate that "something must be earned first before it can be distributed", is wrong. It is a matter of designing policy and the entire economic process right from the start in such a way that the surplus benefits all including the poor. Important elements of such a policy are, for example, land reform and development of finance systems.

RELATIONSHIP OF GROWTH TO POVERTY

According to today's conventional wisdom, income poverty expresses only a part of what poverty means. Not least through the voices of the poor themselves, it has become clear that violation of human dignity and rights, a lack of participation in decisions and exclusion from society, unequal treatment of men and women, and vulnerability are also regarded as poverty. For poverty is caused to a great degree by conflicts of power and interests. Income poverty often is not even seen as the greatest problem.

What relationship do these more far reaching characteristics of poverty have to economic growth? A direct relationship of growth to socially-related aspects such as women's inheritance rights, land rights and exclusion from decisions cannot be seen. Considerable improvements in favour of the poor can be achieved here even without economic growth.

Those who see a strong and causal connection between economic-growth and poverty reduction must ask themselves what the prospects are for high growth rates and thus, for a decline in poverty. Coupling poverty reduction to economic-growth is problematic. If only low growth rates are to be expected.

Another question is whether continuous increases in growth are at all desirable and possible in the medium-to-long-term. In this connection, a difference should perhaps be made between developing countries and industrialised nations. But environmental Compatibility and availability of resources set limits to growth for both. Some academics assume that industralised nations have already reached an inherent limit (stagnation theory) and that the high growth rates of earlier years will not return. Moreover, they add, full employment is no longer achievable due to, among other things, an ongoing increase in productivity, and current unemployment cannot be reduced by customary means. In any case, if growth were to be taken as the major benchmark, the prospects for a radical reduction of income poverty around the world would be modest.

SUMMING UP

Poverty is a complex problem and reducing it depends upon many interconnected factors that is why poverty cannot be attributed to one main cause nor its reduction based on one main strategy. Economic Growth is just one strategic element among many others related to poverty reduction. An indirect causal connection between growth and poverty reduction can only be seen because Governments will have a greater scope for action due to economic-growth, and if they promote labour-intensive development.

Therefore, growth's role in poverty reduction must be put into perspective growth cannot be the first thing that comes to mind, nor is it the golden path to reducing poverty. The simplistic theory of economic growth as the main condition obstructs the bigger picture; it clings to the underlying and ongoing belief in the trickle-down effect. Even if there is no growth or for inherent reasons there can be none, there are promising ways to take on the challenge of mass poverty in the developing countries. Up front, Governments and bilateral and multi-lateral donors must have the political will to design economic, financial and social policies so that they are oriented on poverty in a coherent way—the result can also be economic growth.

21

SEX AND GENDER
(A World of Difference)

Understanding the differences between women and men, and how they are determined, is of key importance in understanding why a gender perspective is so important for development and the elimination of world poverty.

Differences between women and men are determined by biology, on the one hand, and society, on the other:

- Sex marks the distinction between women and men as result of the fundamental biological, physical and genetic differences between them.
- Gender roles are set by convention and other social, economic, political and cultural forces.

The precise boundary between these factors is the subject of fierce debate. Some people believe that the only important difference is that women can bear children and men cannot. Others believe that biology determines a much wider set of characteristics, attributes, and capabilities. Whatever the case, the wide variation in the position of women in different societies around the world demonstrates that, unlike sex, gender roles are by no means fixed by nature—they are made by people, and can be renegotiated and changed.

The position of women in society is far from being of academic interest alone. It not only has fundamental consequences for the quality of life of both women and men, but also has a direct impact on a society's prosperity and well being. The Government's Policy on International Development recognises that gender-based inequality is a major obstacle to the escape from poverty. Studies have shown that developing countries which strive to ensure that women have equal rights have higher rates of economic growth, lower mortality rates, smaller and healthier families, and a better-educated population. Changing gender roles can make a world of difference.

The evidence also shows that gender equality is not a luxury which can only be afforded by rich countries. UN data reveals that some developing countries outperform much richer ones in the opportunities they afford women. The better performing countries are scattered throughout the world, showing that culture and religion need not be barriers to the advancement of women.

The gender gap in many countries is closing fast. Rapid progress has been made in recent decades. But in no society do women fare as well as men. Women are gaining ground in health and education terms, but still have a long way to go in sharing political and economic opportunities. They continue to suffer high levels of violence and abuse, and in many countries are treated differently to men by the law. These disadvantages are not due to sex differences, but are the result of gender discrimination.

EMPOWERMENT, EQUALITY, AND EQUITY: WHAT DO THEY MEAN?

Women's empowerment, gender equality and equity are key terms in debates about the changes required in the relationships between women and men.

- *Empowerment* means individuals acquiring the power to think and act freely, exercise choice, and to fulfil their potential as full and equal members of society.
- *Equality* means that women should have the same rights and entitlements as men to human, social, economic and cultural development, and equal voice in civil and

political life. It does not mean that everyone should be the same, or that the benefits of development should be shared in exactly equal proportions by everyone. This would be neither feasible nor desirable, and would not be consistent with the notion of empowerment, which upholds everyone's right to determine their own future and the lifestyle of their choice.

- *Equity* means that the exercise of these rights should lead to outcomes which are fair and just, and which enable women to have the same power as men to define and pursue the objectives of development and shape societies of the future.

The difference between equality and equity is important because it underlines the rights of women to define the objectives of development for themselves, and to seek outcomes which are not necessarily identical to those sought or enjoyed by men. Women have the right to pursue development paths which reflect their own needs and aspirations.

Upholding these rights is in the interests of men as well as women, because of the wider social and economic benefits brought by gender equality. Because of the universal disadvantages experienced by women, their empowerment is crucial to the achievement of equality and equity, the elimination of poverty and a better world for all.

22

TOBIN TAX

James Tobin, a Nobel laureate in economics, dreamt up his idea for a 'Tobin Tax' in the 1960s when the gold exchange standard was still in force. Before long the US closed the gold window at the Federal Reserve, giving rise to the current regime of floating currencies. Tobin argued that speculative flows of 'hot money' would put unwanted pressure on fixed exchange rates not reflecting economic fundamentals, and would upset macro-economic management he thought that if purchases and sales of foreign currency were subject to a small tax (a fraction of 1 per cent of the value of each transaction), long-term investment and current account operations would not be significantly affected, but currency speculators conducting large volumes of transactions adding upto a high value would be deterred.

The Tobin Tax has never been implemented and was largely forgotten until in the mid-1990s. The late Mahbut ul haq and his fellow authors of the United Nations Development Programme's annual Human Development Report then revived the idea with a view not so much to calming fever in the international Capital Market as raising extra resources to finance development. Now, War on Want is echoing this call in its report Costing the Casino: The Real impact of Currency Speculation in the 1990s.

Currency speculation plays a central role in global instability which in turn brings increased poverty and instability to

Developing Countries, argues War on want. Its report shows, for example, that the delayed effects of the South East Asia economic crisis in 1997-98 continue to hit the poor.

At a time of declining official flows, Developing Countries rely more and more on private capital flows to finance their growth. Their dependence on volatile, short-term investment exposes their fragile economies to sudden changes in financial markets. The frequency of financial crises around the world in itself urges measures to stabilise this volatility

A Tobin Tax could help deter speculation by making currency trading more costly, in particular it would act to deter short-term transactions of large sums between countries more expensive.

Another advantage of the Tax, says War on Want, is its revenue-raising potential-particularly in view of the 'current diminishing scale of aid budgets'. The organisation believes the threat of further economic crises, as in South East Asia, makes the adoption-or at least consideration—of a Tobin Tax 'a matter of some urgency',

However, its critics say the Tobin Tax raises a number of thorny questions: Does it make economic sense? The consensus view of economists is that markets, including capital markets, work best if information is good, transaction costs are minimised and distractions removed. The Tobin Tax would introduce an, albeit small, transaction cost and distraction. True capital markets are subject to bubbles and panics. But taxes are not the way to deal with these. Instead, there needs to be better supervision of markets and institutions, with occasional official (or IMF) intervention to preserve stability?

Would the Tobin tax work? If applied, it would almost certainly be subject to massive avoidance as Tax-liable transactions were relocated in financial centres whose authorities had not agreed to implement the Tax. There are no internationally-recognised means of obliging countries to raise a tax. Furthermore, there is a very rapidly increasing volume of transactions in foreign exchange derivatives-futures, options and swaps. It is not clear if these would be taxed also.

Would the Tax raise significant resources for development? Very large sums could theoretically be raised if foreign exchange markets all applied the tax and if there were no avoidance, and if the Governments which collected the Tax were willing to devote the proceeds to aid. But Governments have no overriding reason to hypothecate the revenue from any particular source to aid (why not devote the proceeds of airport Departure Tax to aid?)

According to its critics, the Tobin. Tax was not a very good idea for achieving its original purpose of calming speculations, for both theoretical and practical reasons. Nor is it a good idea as a source of more aid for the same practical reasons (is it workable?). Even if these were overcome it would require the assent and collaboration of the very Governments whose current decisions to provide aid (or not) have hitherto determined the magnitude of aid flows.

23

AFTER THE MICROCREDIT SUMMIT
(How to Implement Its Anti-Poverty Strategy)

More than 2500 people from 100 countries gathered in Washington in February, 1997, to participate in the Microcredit Summit. The goal of the organizers of the Summit is to reach 100 million poor families around the world with microcredits and other financial services within the next ten years. As there are at least six people in a family, 600 million people would benefit from access to micro finance. This means that half of the people in extreme poverty could have the opportunity to get out of their misery.

The fact that more than one billion people in the world are still living in extreme poverty is a sign of failure of our development-policy and a scandal for human society. Now there is no longer any excuse. We have learned in the last years that microcredit is one of the best tools to eradicate poverty. At the Summit, there was a consensus between politicians, practitioners, donors, scientists and NGOS on how to reach this goal. Particular emphasis is given to strengthening poor people in their capacities. It is also understood that lack of funds is only one aspect of the most pressing problems in the field of microfinance.

THE APPROACH

The overall goal can be achieved by designing and establishing an appropriate and sustainable institutional framework on the national level in the Developing Countries. The most significant elements within a feasible strategy to achieve the goal are the following:

- Decentralized, bilateral fund-raising and financing under commonly accepted standards are preferred, whereas the creation of a new global facility as a supranational mobilizing and channelling mechanism for microcredit should not be pursued.
- The focal point of the future strategy should be the creation and the support of independent and recipient countries which will operate under the basic principles of outreach. Moreover, the mobilization of domestic funds will be of particular importance. Promoting agencies as wholesale institutions should identify and assess eligible microfinance institutions on the basis of a widely accepted set of performance criteria, identify institutional weakness and requirements at national level and execute programmes for the funding, institutional strengthening, training and linking of participating institutions.
- The NGO *Results*, which helped organize the Microcredit Summit, will perform as a catalyst in creating public awareness regarding the crucial role of microfinance in poverty alleviation in donor as well as recipient countries.
- The Consultative Group to Assist the Poorest (CGAP) will be responsible for the creation of promoting agencies at the national level. The role of CGAP will be the monitoring and coordinating of promotional activities. It will act as a platform for setting consistent standards for the operation of individual programmes.

THE NEXT STEPS

Under the guidance of CGAP, interested donor and recipient countries should immediately begin to discuss the institutional profiles of promoting agencies and performance criteria of participating institutions. Moreover, the necessary operational procedures for the functioning of the institutional framework at the wholesale level need to be defined by CGAP. CGAP should identify promoting agencies within the next six months. It will be responsible for the coordination of funding activities. Capacity building for promoting agencies as well as for recipient institutions will be a crucial issue. A pilot phase in a small number of countries should be designed to gain experience with the proposed institutional framework in order to develop it further, and also determine the adequate volume of funding for potential recipient institutions. Bilateral donors should support these activities.

24

ON THE WAY TO COMMERCIAL MICROCREDITS

(The Changing of a Development Instrument)

The founding of financial institutions in the Developing Countries, whose target groups are supposed to be poorer people and, in particular, income-generating micro, small-scale and medium-sized enterprises, originated in the industrialised nations. Soon after Western "Development Policy" began in the 1950s and 1960s the donors noted that investment in infrastructure was insufficient to achieve growth. Reflecting on the experiences of Europe, state or mixed-enterprise Development Banks were founded in many Developing Countries with the support of various donors. The banks were to promote industrialisation as a substitution for imports, as well as farming, housing construction and regional development. Their common feature was that they combined the characteristics of a bank and a public authority. On the one hand, they managed loan holdings and handled payment transactions, and one the other they "prompted" development by non-repayable grants. Since these functions each followed a very different logic, the banks were required to undertake a difficult tightrope walk.

EXCLUSION OF SMALL BORROWERS

As a justification for the existence of state banks, even in liberal market economies people like to point out, and rightly so, that normal commercial banks would have scarcely any interest in the business of the "small fry" and, that they also shun longer-term financing of investment. A lender cannot beforehand tell the difference between good and less good borrowers, and must set a uniform interest rate for his credit offer. In order not to lose his cost-efficient and low risk customer's, meaning to avoid what the economists call "adverse selection", he sets the interest rate not as high as he would have to in covering his costs in the case of small borrowers, and "rations" his loans according to criteria such as reputation, collateral and business volume, Even in an otherwise completely liberalised model world, small borrowers, remain excluded from formal bank loans even if they would be able and prepared to bear cost-covering terms. That applies to an even because, other being equal, in most countries of the world they have lower incomes than men and also are discriminated against in access to property rights.

Therefore, in micro-economic terms, the idea behind the founding of Development Banks is well-founded. However, the design of the institutional structures, including the governance structure, requires a fine balancing of the bank and public authority functions in order to reconcile efficiency, cost- covering and the promotion mission. All too often, the easy way out for all involved is to combine the negative features of bank and public authority, meaning linking profit-mongering and the exclusion of small borrowers with a subsidy mentality and politisation. As critical studies from the 1970s showed, following the initial euphoria, development banks seldom live up to their promises.

For the donor institutions, however, these banks are ideal counterparts absorbing financial and technical assistance. Thanks to their banking function in payment transactions, they practically never have outflow problems. In addition, they can at any time produce from their broad portfolios the projects demanded by a donor or; his client, such as Parliamentary Committee. And promoting Development Banks also promotes the exports of the donors, meaning the industrialised nations.

An important point of criticism focuses on this "hidden" promotion of exports. This is that micro, small-scale and medium-size enterprises mostly do not need a great deal of imports, and especially not so long as they are still building a trusting relationship with their bank to overcome the asymmetrical information mentioned above. So they need loans in local rather than foreign currency.

When favourably-priced foreign currency; loans are available for projects which a bank public authority or company would in any case implement or promote, these can be used for other purposes, such as for imports of consumer goods or other agreeable things which otherwise could not be afforded. So who can blame politicians, bureaucrats, bank directors or companies when they prove to be fervent supporters of the financing of development banks!

Critics of the development bank system did not have an easy task in asserting themselves against the concerted interest of individuals on both the donor and recipient sides. But the search for alternatives began on a broad front in the 1980s.

ALTERNATIVES TO DEVELOPMENT BANK PROMOTION

Committed politicians, bureaucrats, academics, consultants and NGOs in various countries around the world began to get down to serious work in forming a new policy. Their efforts were based on the declared principles of poverty alleviation and sustainability in institution-building in promoting micro, small-scale and medium scale enterprises via the finance sector. The results were published in the World Bank's World Development Report of 1989.

In an initial step, so-called "integrated" rural and urban projects and programmes were equipped with their own "rotation funds". Which were to finance employment and income-generating measures. However, due to their integration in projects focussed on infrastructure measures such as slum clearance, irrigation, electrification, public health services and regional planning, they degenerated typically into drawing funds for projects management's. That meant that a recipient mentality rather than a sustainable financial service provider structure came into being, and the mixing of loans and free gifts undermined rather than promoted a positive attitude towards market-conform financial relationships.

The Grameena Bank in Bangladesh is a special case. Here, the charismatic professor Muhammed Yunus persuaded the Government to place a state bank in the service of poverty alleviation, and for landless women in particular. The results are not undisputed, especially since the bank is still very dependent upon subsidies. But this institution shows that participation in the monetary economy is anything but a matter of course, and that emancipation of women as free economic citizens is a goal to which purely technological financial principles should perhaps be subordinated. The Grameena Bank has yet to stand the test of developing into a sustainable institution without a heroic head and without subsides. Maybe it will really show now a poor country like Bangladesh can establish itself in the long term as a "funnel" for permanent development assistance transfers. But a final assessment does not appear to be possible at present.

The NGOs are another alternative to customary Development Banks. Donors like to promote them because they are close to the target groups, or at least are able to portray themselves so. In practice, however, they prove to be problematical partners when it comes to developing a durable formal finance structure in the interests of small borrowers. As committed left-wingers, NGO members and leaders usually take a sceptical stance towards the market and its "bourgeois" laws. They are seldom willing to act as bankers with all necessary toughness and assume the "ownership" of a financial institution.

Critical evaluations show that in some case NGOs can be persuaded to found financial institutions and also run them as sole or co-owners. But the success of such upgrading projects depends very much upon the consultants and donors, and above all upon the existence of a capable leader. They cannot, however, be regarded as a norm.

The target groups and the academics advising them on-site noticed after a while, of course, that the big words were hollow. They realised that first and foremost it was matter of the hidden agenda of the national and international financiers and not particularly about reducing poverty among the target groups. If the "frontier" of the formal finance sector was to be pushed downwards in the direction of the poor, what they really needed in financial services had to be made available to them. These were small, readily available operating funds and emergency loans and secure and worthwhile investment options for temporary financial surpluses. Since poverty was a mass phenomenon, these financial products had to be offered with a loan technology, meaning a form of organisation, that gave them a mass reach with as much saturation as possible.

The then prevailing pattern was "controlled investment loan", involving obligatory consultancy, subsidised interest rates and relatively large sums to push through innovations in the context of "Pilot Projects" which, however, due to limited subsidy funds, never got beyond the promotion of a few "pilots". So the reforms diagnosis meant a radical change. But there were enough people on either side of the political "barricades" who became convinced by this plausible if hardy grandiose concept. As a self-supporting commercial system which nevertheless was in the interests of the target groups, it began to assert itself towards the end of the 1990s under the label of "commercial approach" or "new development finance".

AFTER THE FALL OF THE BERLIN WALL

With the fading of utopic vision, empirically-based diagnoses gained ground and showed that precisely an unpretentious and reliable bank-customer relationship was the best contribution a bank could make to economic survival. In addition, they also demonstrated that in many cases a bank could in fact also help the target group of poor people, and particularly micro—and small-scale enterprises, to accumulate assets. Furthermore, it should be not only be mentioned but even emphasised that there were, and should be, public services of all kinds, including old age pensions, family allowance and similar transfers. Which counter poverty around the world. That was necessary to prevent microcredit programmes and similar bank services facing a demand they could not meet. Taking out a loan and servicing it with interest and repayment of the capital sum is always a burden for the borrower, and possible a benefit only in so far as it enables a special opportunity for profit to be seized. For the poorest of the poor, transfers are called for not loans and other bank or insurance services.

Development co-operation practicians on the ground and ideologically unbiased theorists alike came to these conclusions as early as the mid-1980s. But the ideological pressure did not ease until after the collapse of the East Bloc, when both the communist threat and the Utopia of the non-capitalist workers' and farmers paradise disappeared.

So it is not surprising that shortly afterwards the practicians of both sides and the immediate representatives of the target groups got together with enlightened representatives of donors, consultants and academics to form an international coalition titled "New Development Finance". The Microcredit Summit of 1997 with Hillary Clinton had already leaned in this direction, even if it still sent no clear signal in regard to the issue of dependency on subsidies. But the donors gave a green light for a massive financial promotion. World Bank president James Wolfensohn promised that together with all the other summit participants he would go all to ensure that by 2005 an additional 100 million families around the world would have microcredits.

The subsequent "Annual Conferences on New Development Finance", which took place at the University of Frankfurt? Main from 1997 to 1999, then developed into an important forum at which formerly diametrically opposed actors joined forces against the "ancient regime", According to their definition, "old" is everything which boils down to the demand of re-educating people and coupling loans with obligatory consultancy. In the long term, that results in dependency on subsidies, becoming hostage to the political games of influential national rulers and donors, and loses sight of the declared target group of the urban and rural poor. All this applies mainly to smaller countries which receive heavy international assistance. In India,

Pakistan and Brazil, not to mention China, the conditions have their own rhythms and special features.

After the end of communism there was a new situation not only in the Developing Countries and the North-South relationship, but also and above all in Eastern Europe. Established donor institutions such as USAID and the Reconstruction Loan Corporate (KfW) were supplemented by the multilateral European Bank for Reconstruction and Development (EBRD), and what were soon to be called "transformation Countries" lined up with the "classic" recipients of International Development Aid.

Internationally operating NGOs and consultancies with experience if the microcredit systems of Developing Countries were not also called for to assist the projects and programmes in Eastern Europe. The finance sector was perceived as the core of every market economy. At the same time, the donors soon recognised the importance of small to medium-sized business, trades, small holders and all the many disparate micro and small-scale enterprises for employment and the supply of the population However, financial services were not available to any great degree to cover their needs.

It could now be seen that payment transactions did not function without commercial banks, and that this shortcoming had a considerable negative impact on small enterprises. Going beyond microcredits, which until then had always been the main instrument of financial assistance, the focus was now on deposits, transfers and all the other financial services that were important for the target groups. "Microfinancing" gradually became the generic term for the orientation of financial sector measures to benefit the "small people".

DOWN-SCALING" OR "STARTING FROM SCRATCH"

By means of special loan programmes, which were kept separate from the other portfolios, the external donors sought at first to persuade the existing banks to downscale their activities and address the newly emerging small to medium-size businesses in the private sector. On balance, the result was rather meager, for these programmes did little to influence the characteristics of the major Eastern European Commercial Banks. And every time some of them were privatised or had to be shut down due to financial rows or corruption scandals, it affected the special small enterprises portfolios regardless of how, efficiently they were managed.

Besides using this channel via the big banks, donors also began building up loan programmes through NGOs and local chambers of commerce. The result here were also disappointing, for local implementing organisations are mostly unsuitable for a substansible mass banking business.

But senior officials and executive at donors and consultancies soon had the idea of founding their own micro-finance institutes. "Starting from scartch" green field banking and similar terms began to make the rounds The first "Micro-Enterprise Bank" came into being in Bosnia and soon afterwards other Micro-Finance Institutions (MFIs) were founded.

Unlike customary development cooperation projects, which have a time-frame, the MFIs are open-ended, and consultants in the North also see themselves as long-term partner. In contrast, International Development Organisations are more and more becoming second-class partners from which local bodies must sooner or later separate themselves again to avoid being left in the lurch. After all, their cooperation has a time limit, and they will leave the country again

In view of the challenges of globalisation, the banks should perhaps consider using their development projects to establish a network of long-term investments and thus, fulfil their promotion mission in favour of the "small people" not only locally and nationally, but also globally.

25

SMALL PEOPLE'S BANKS

(The Role of Micro-Enterprise Banks in Development Assistance)

Micro-Enterprise Banks (MEBs) grant many small loans, offer investment opportunities, and handle their customer's payment transactions at home and abroad. They are licensed by and under the control of local banking supervisory bodies. They are growing fast and expanding their branch networks.

Direct observation and simple arithmetic show that the banks make a substantial contribution to local finance systems and thus, to their countries' economic development. Their input to development is socially relevant above all because they offer their services first and foremost to the kinds of customers in which existing local banks appear to have no interest. A part from the jobs in the small enterprises they finance, the banks themselves offer many young people skilled employment. In addition, thee small banks make a profit. They also have private investors, who are becoming more and more important to them.

All that appears to be quite astonishing, most of all perhaps because MEB are founded as development assistance projects. A consensus has emerged in development cooperation in recent years in which institutions such as MEB appear to be a new model. The MEBs are the newcomers on this list, and their success can already be noted from their figures. A more precise analysis seeking to isolate the quantitative influence of their various success factors, including that of donor inputs, would require more data than is available due to the newness of the MEBs . But what already appears to be clear is that establishing new banks is a promising new approach in the microfinance sector.

LEARNING FROM EXPERIENCE

The new approach is an attempt to draw lessons from the positive and negative experiences of financing development and implement them. An initial and very positive lesson relates to the methods of granting loans. It is indeed possible to grant, with tolerable costs and a very low repayment default rate, microcredits to people whom conventional bankers view as not credit worthy and in whom established banks have no interest.

This methodology is neither a secret nor difficult to learn, However, it is not compatible with the organisational structures and processes of customary banks, which are focused on other business fields and target groups. That is the second lesson, drawn from many so-called downscaling projects. To be successful at granting small-scale and micro-loans, a bank must be capable and willing to go in for far-reaching decentralisation of decision-making agree to performance related pay, and offer skilled employees credible job and promotion prospects. And to achieve that the bank must also grow. As a counterbalance to decentralisation bank staff must be very well trained and highly motivated, and sophisticated control mechanisms must be in place.

These considerations are good reasons for offering financial services for "small" people through special institutions. This was attempted in the past by the strategy of upgrading existing loan granting NGOs by external support. The experiences with upgrading were in part very good, but some of them were problematical.

The third lesson is clearly positive. It is indeed possible, with acceptable expenditure of development assistance funds to upgrade on existing institution and transform it into an efficient bank for "small" customers. And that brings us to the fourth and rather negative lesson. Upgrading has inherent limits. Positions based on power and self-interest arise in the process of developing and promoting existing institutions, and they obstruct a project's progress. The manager or founder/ initiator of an externally promoted and relatively successful loan-granting NGO naturally has little interest in his or her institution becoming a "proper bank" for whose management they would not be suitable, if due only to the banking supervisory body's qualification requirements. The donors, too, who usually have financed the expensive first stage of an upgrading process, regrettably often do not see themselves as owners and advocates of the promoted institutions and, above all, of the target groups they have not yet reached. As a rule they are satisfied with what has been achieved. They avoid a confrontation with those who defend their positions and thereby impede further development of the institution, even if this is desirable in developmental terms.

It is precisely successful institution—strengthening that aggravates the dichotomy between those who have attained influential and prestigious positions and want to protect their interests and the interests of the target groups and the bank's employees in expanding the institution. This conflict, for which there is plenty of empirical proof, has a structural cause. NGOs have no owners that have an '"objective" interest in the long-term financial and developmental success of the projects and will therefore, assume a constructive role. Formalising the institution changes nothing so long as there is not at the same time a substantial change in the ownership structure.

SETTING UP NEW MICROFINANCE BANKS

The new approach differs in two respects from customary institution building by upgrading. First, the phases of institution strengthening ahead of formalising and transforming are leapfrogged. Instead of expanding and converting an NGO, it is about setting up a new micro-finance bank. Second, the issue of ownership and Governance are clarified from the start based on the perspective cf medium-term development. But the more technical problems of granting loans and the design of the institution can be solved largely according to proven models.

Setting up a bank from scratch in a developing or transformation country involves a number of steps. The first is project identification. The main question here is whether the project could make developmental sense. The second step is to assess whether a new bank is really necessary and meaningful in developmental terms, economically sound and politically feasible, Economic soundness is assessed under the assumption that for the initial phase technical assistance and refinancing of the first loans on favourable terms can be procured. Without these, the projects could not be implemented at precisely the time when they appeared to be particularly important for development.

In the third step, provisional consensus must be reached among potential investors and the so-called sponsor, who is to build-up the bank in technical terms and manage it during its early days. In addition, knock-on financing from one or more donors must be secured. What is decisive for potential inclusion as an international investor is first to be willing and able to play an active role as an owner and be present on the board of the new bank. The second requirement is to contribute to the success of the project above and beyond having a capital stake in it. The third condition is to share the concept of a commercially oriented strategy of institution building that is nevertheless committed to development.

The second condition can be fulfilled by, for example, an investor also functioning as a donor and providing Technical Cooperation funds or loans or procuring them from pure donors. If the other two conditions were not met, coordination would be too difficult. The group of possible investors who fulfill as the perquisites is very limited. Investors who had only capital to offer would be quite easy to find. But including them in the setting-up phase would only hamper coordination. In principle, the development institutions are possible project sponsors, who should also be investors. But in practice there is more a tendency to call in a private company with relevant experience.

The fourth step is to develop a business plan. This forms the basis for a binding commitment by the investors, the sponsors and, if applicable, the donors. The plan also covers the founding of a local company as the legal entity responsible for the future bank, the application for a bank license, and the technical preparation for opening the bank including recruiting and training local staff.

If the entire process is completed quickly, it takes a year. Based on experienced, compared with upgrading projects the time needed for setting up a functioning bank is shorter, the cost to donors lower and the chances of success greater.

SUCCESS DEPENDS ON NATURAL TRUST AND EXPERIENCE

The success of the new banks promotes their employee's commitment and loyalty and strengthens the link between investors and sponsors. It thereby reinforce precisely the factors that are required of them to allow this success to occur. That is why time and gain the same actors get together in various projects as international investors, sponsors and donors. All parties must know each other well and have well-founded trust in each other for last and successful handling of the process. And only a rapid sequence of similar projects involving the same actors offers the opportunity of transferring knowledge, including qualified staff, from one "building site" to the next. Where if not in similar projects, can someone who is to set up and manage a microfinance bank or their' loans department learn how to do it? Where, other than in a "sister" project, is local staff to be trained before the bank is opened? Where, other than in similar and effectively linked banks, are there the opportunities of advancement, which must be offered, to the best local staff in order to strengthen their motivation and retain them?

26

CAUGHT IN THE DEBT TRAP?

(The Foreign Indebtedness of Developing Countries)

The question of whether there is a way out of the Developing Countries Debt Trap can only be properly answered if their indebtedness is not viewed as an isolated factor. It should be seen in the context of the total net resource flows into these countries. The following facts must be borne in mind:

1. Net resource flows to Developing Countries increased from 1994 to 1995 by 11.5 per cent to US per cent 231.3 bn. The greatest share was made up of private sector flows, which accounted for 72 per cent ($ 167.1 bn) of total transfer inputs.

2. Of the private flows, foreign direct investments totalling $90.3 bn dominate. Their well above average increase reflects the globalisation of production and growing integration of developing and transformation countries in the World Economy. To date, however, this has applied mainly to 12 countries on which about 80 per cent of private inflows is concentrated. These are China, Mexico, Brazil, South Korea, Malaysia, Argentina, Indonesia, Thailand, Russia, India, Turkey and Hungary.

3. Portfolio equity flows to developing countries known for their high sensitivity on earnings and policy have dropped markedly for the time being to $ 22 bn. This is a not unexpected reaction to:

- the sharp rise in US interest rates since February 1994 and a very positive trend on the American capital market;
- the Mexican Peso crisis which began in December 1994; and
- the more cautious evaluation of the risks of investments in emerging markets, which major institutional investors believe have reached a certain degree of saturation.

4. Official development finance totalled $ 64.2 bn, of which, the World Bank reported, $ 11 bn was allocated to the rescue action for Mexico alone. ODA in 1995 stagnated at $ 47 bn. Its proportion of the 'OECD donor countries' GDPs was 0.29 per cent, the lowest since the beginning of the 1970s. The main reasons for this downturn were the industrial nations' well-known public budget problems and the fact that more creditworthy development and transformation countries are increasingly procuring their finance on private capital markets. Understandably, large sums were made available, mainly by Germany, to Eastern Europe and the successor states to the former Soviet Union. From strictly developmental view-points, it is disquieting that ever fewer ODA funds are available for longer-term development projects due to their disbursement for short-term emergency and crisis assistance.

THE WASHINGTON DECISIONS

The recent annual conference of G-7 Finance Ministers and Central Bank Chiefs took the following decisions:

1. About 20 Highly Indebted Poor Countries (HIPCs) were to be reviewed to establish whether in endeavouring to solve their debt problems they could expect greater support from the international donor community than previously. There was a justified fear that without enhanced assistance, and continuing to employ only the instruments used to date, these countries would not

even achieve an acceptable level of indebtedness within the next 5-10 years.

2. *Time horizon*: in two three-year stages, a comprehensive review of the indebtedness and adjustment measures the affected countries could cope with would be undertaken. This would include observing the impacts of employing the customary instruments of debt relief. If the results were unsatisfactory, the new measures decided in Washington, which were expected to achieve a positive breakthrough, would be applied as well after three to six years. In detail, these are:

   - *Paris Club* (*Official Creditors*): rescheduling of bilateral debts, with case-to-case remission of up to 80 per cent compared with a current ceiling of 67 per cent;
   - Comparable relief conditions through non-Paris Club and private creditors (London Club);
   - *IMF*: grants from the Enhanced Structural Adjustment Facility (ESAF) or long-term ESAF loans. The recipient countries to use these sums for debt servicing; and
   - Redemption of multilateral debts from a future HIPC trust fund to be administered by the IDA. Setting up the fund will formally ensure that it is not a matter of debt remission.

3. *Financing*: provisional estimates put the cost of the HIPC initiative at around $ 6 bn. This is to be funded by the Paris Club members, third-party creditors and international finance institutions. Two factors of the total costs are uncertain.

   These are the number of countries which in the end will be given access to the funds, and the realism of the estimates of export income upon which the country analyses are based.

4. *Assessment*: all in all, the HIPC initiative is a fresh attempt to substantially relieve these countries of their

debt problems, and support their economic reform programmes and measures to alleviate poverty. The World Bank and IMF were directed to begin implementing the debt initiative without delay and report back to the conference of the supervisory bodies in the spring of this year. Leading donor countries were able to agree to the initiative because:

- financial integrity, particularly the preferential creditor status of the World Bank, the IMF and the Regional Development Banks, was not in question.
- the debtor countries were not relieved of their basic responsibility for comprehensive and sustainable adjustment policies; and finally.
- the usual case-to-case procedure, taking decisions from country to country, was retained.

GLOBAL IMPACTS

To complete the "indebtedness picture", two other important problem areas must be pointed out. The problems and risks arising from the HIPCs' indebtedness affect first and foremost the national and, at worst, the regional level of the countries concerned. A serious endangering of the global finance and currency system must not be allowed to emanate from them. However, and this is the first problem, it can be much graver in the case of advanced Developing Countries, as Mexico showed in 1995. The risks which arise for the money and capital markets from liberalisation of short-term movements of capital in a number of threshold countries with large issue volumes are considerable Strictly speaking, the capital market securities acquired in these markets by nationals and foreigners are only partly foreign debts. However, because they can be sold at any time and their convertibility and transferability is guaranteed, they can present similarly high risks for the solvency of the country concerned as "traditional" foreign debts. Additionally, the fact that "maturity" here depends not on contractually agreed terms, but on fragile investor confidence, enhances, the risks.

The large sums deployed in the Mexico rescue action organised by the USA and IMF show that endangerment of the international finance system was on hand. Above all, what the financial world aptly labelled the "Tequila effect"—a chain reaction of investors making a mass flight out of other threshold countries such as Brazil, Argentina and the Philippines, which threatened to spread—called for comprehensive confidence-building measures.

Not least, this experience was the basis for the agreement by the G-7 Ministers and Central Bankers in Washington on initial steps of a new IMF crisis financing mechanisms. Thus, the General Agreement on Credits was doubled to Special Drawing Rights of $ 34 bn.

CONCLUSIONS

The conclusions that must be drawn from this development are:

- to strengthen the IMF's role as a catalyst and improve its surveillance function;
- to bring the G-7 group in their own interest to put in place stable economic general conditions, above all harmonised control of the interest rates of the key currencies; and
- to support the threshold countries in creating credible political conditions, especially by stabilising their economic, financial and currency policies in order to give no cause for sudden crises of confidence.

27

THIRD WORLD DEBT IS STILL GROWING

Developing Country Debt is estimated to have grown to over $1.8 trillion last year, up from $1.77 trillion in 1994. During the past decade, much of this debt has been restructured-renegotiated on terms more favourable to debtor countries. Some 80 per cent of the funds owed to Commercial Banks, as well as a much smaller share of loans from Governments and multilateral institutions, have now been restructured. The trend has led some analysts to declare the debt crisis over, at least for the Private Banks. But the poorest nations have yet to see much relief. Their debt service payments still eat up a substantial percentage of their export revenues—some 15 to 19 per cent, depending upon the measurements used. The ratio typical of the era before the crisis began in 1982 was on the order of 10 to 12 per cent.

The worst debt today is that of sub-Saharan Africa, excluding South Africa. Collectively the region's debt amounts to $ 180 billion, three times the 1980 total, and 10 per cent higher than its entire output of goods and services. Debt service payments come to $ 10 billion annually, about four times what the region spends on health and education combined. The burden is choking off economic development over much of the continent.

Eastern Europe and the countries of the former Soviet Union are also heavily indebted, but the picture varies considerably from one country to another. The region's total debt rose from 161 per cent of export earnings in 1986 to an estimated 291 per cent last year. Russia owes over $ 80 billion, and the country is hard pressed to meet its obligations: interest payments in 1994 were budgeted at less than 15 per cent of interest due. Poland, on the other hand, had 40 per cent of its debt forgiven in a restructuring agreement last year. Half of Bulgaria's debt was forgiven in 1993.

In Latin America, restructuring has eased the burdens of three major borrowers—Mexico, Argentina and Brazil. Peru is the region's last remaining country with significant unrestructured debt. Peru's debt currently amounts to $ 26 billion.

Restructuring has brought some new actors onto the scene- and changed the roles of established players. After shedding much of the "old." high-risk debt of the 1980s, the commercial banks are moving aggressively into lucrative east Asian markets, and into private sector lending in Latin America. This more selective lending has allowed American banks, for instance, to post a 17 per cent increase in Third World loans over the year ending last March, and a 33 per cent increase since 1990.

As private lending goes elsewhere, the poorest countries have had to rely increasingly on multilateral institutions like the World Bank and the International Monetary Fund. Multilateral debt among the lowest income countries grew from around 15 per cent of total debt in 1980 to over 24 per cent in 1992. Multilateral loans generally come with much stricter terms. Neither, the World Bank nor the IMF will directly forgive or restructure debt, since that might jeopardize their "preferred status" in capital markets and force them to raise interest rates. Their preferred status also means that payments to these institutions take precedence over payments to all other creditors. Of the various types of external debt, multilateral loans generally have the most rigid terms.

The multilaterals do, however, participate in a form of restructuring by providing most of the financing for "Brady" bonds, used to restructure the old debt of "middle income" countries like brazil, Mexico, and Argentina. But the bonds are not available to the poorest countries.

Organizations that aren't in the business of lending money have become involved in restructuring as well, through swap agreements. Debt swaps reduce the amount owed in return for some concession on the part of the debtor. In debt for—equity swaps, for example, a corporation purchases a debtor nation's IOU from a band, and then trades it for one of the country's state-owned assets, such as a steel mill or a telephone company Debt or equity swaps are often part of a larger privatization strategy, especially in Latin America. While privatization may often be necessary for saving nationalized industries, many observers are concerned that indebtedness is forcing countries to part with their assets at "fire sale" prices. Between 1985 and 1992, debt-for-equity swaps accounted for nearly 36 per cent of all debt conversions.

Debt-for-nature and debt-for-development swaps are intended to win Government commitments to environmental and Development Projects. In these arrangements, a Non-Governmental Organisation (NGO) usually obtains the debtor nation's IOU from a bank at a significant discount The NGO then typically restructures the debt by passing along some of the discount conceded by the bank, accepting payments in local currency, and investing the returns locally, to fund a national part, for instance, or a public health project. Between 1985 and 1992, these types of swaps accounted for only about 2 per cent of debt conversions. But for some countries, they may already be offering significant relief: Madagascar has cut its $ 100 million Commercial Bank debt in half through debt-for-nature swaps.

28

OVERCOMING THE POVERTY IN INDIA AND THE LESSONS LEARNED

Basic elements in the struggle against poverty in India are the provision of the economic services and assets which the poor have tended not to receive in the pastas a result of oversight or design. The emphasis on economic services and assets is just because the mass of the rural poor are self-employed, and it is upon the improvement in the means of production directly accessible to them that their prosperity depends. Health and education are very important, but offer more if combined with the material means of making a living—of putting body and mind to work. These assets and services include land, water, technology, commercial services handling output and inputs, and credit—provided within an economic policy framework conductive to their optimal exploitation.

This list is hardly new. It corresponds to the requirements of any producer. The basic points to be made in this regard are: firstly, that the general requirements of poor producers are precisely the same as those of other producers and that measures to alleviate poverty that fall short of recognizing the full range of such requirements are doomed to failure; and, secondly, that these assets and services are not typically provided in a form accessible to the poor. India has made important progress in providing a more effective framework for agricultural production "in general", this frame-work has not properly embraced small and poor producers. They are as follows:

ACCESS TO LAND AND WATER

In the case of access to land, for example, land reform efforts in India has frequently involved major loop-holes, allowing the socially powerful to minimize de facto improvements in the condition of the poor. In the critical area of land rights, registration processes have been so complex and costly relative to the resources of the poor that land regularization programmes have, sometimes unintentionally, become virtual characters for legalizing the eviction of the poor and the actual loss of their traditional rights. Irrigation without specific measures to defend the interests of existing occupants of areas exposes them to expulsion—and, moreover, has tended to be concentrated in large-scale schemes benefiting already high potential areas in which the better-off predominate. While huge sums have been spent on large-scale irrigation schemes, little has been spent on water conservation and the sort of small-scale developments that are more likely to be of relevance to marginal small-scale producers.

TECHNOLOGY TRANSFER

In the area of technology, attention has been focused on technologies (such as the Green Revolution) requiring extensive access to water and fertilizers, neither of which are generally available among the poor. In fact, research almost everywhere has concentrated on larger-scale production in areas of relatively high resource endowment. In contrast to this, research relevant to small-scale producers in marginal soil and rainfed areas in India has been shockingly deficient. As in other fields, this is partly explicable in terms of a frequently unproved belief that large-scale production is more efficient. It is also explicable in terms of the fact that it is the powerful who set the research agenda, not the poor. Taking its inspiration from highly specialized, large-scale agricultural units of production, research has tended to dwell separately on individual crops—rather than on the interaction between crops, which is of much greater relevance to small-scale producers engaging in highly complex systems of production to maximize food self-sufficiency and minimize risks.

COMMERCIAL SERVICES

In the area of handling of output and inputs, organized services (not infrequently under public control in the past) have tended to concentrate in the proximity of large-scale producers and users of input in relatively well-endowed areas. In India the poor have had to incur the extraordinary costs of handling their own transport of goods to and from service points—frequently over long and deficient lines of communication. The alternative has been to resort to private intermediaries offering goods, and buying products, at prices very different from those enjoyed by larger producers. In effect, the better-off and the poor have confronted different sets of prices—with the poor paying more for what they buy, and receiving less for what they sell.

CREDIT

In the area of credit, the situation has been disastrous. It is generally recognised that productive improvement needs a change in means of production—new tools, improved seeds, fertilizers, etc. Such a change everywhere is typically effected on the basis of credit. Yet rural credit schemes in India have usually not extended support to small farmers and the poor. Credit has been concentrated among richer farmers with collateral, and with demand for larger loans. In order to improve their productivity, the poor have been forced to seek credit from informal money lenders—at virtually confiscatory rates.

Again, the cost of modernization has been much higher for the poor than for the better-off. The inevitable result has been a lower rate of change—and the consolidation, rather than the reduction of poverty.

THE VICTIMS BLAMED

Although, vast amounts of money have been invested in rural development in India, very little of it has reached the poor. The poor have been left to their own devices, while the better-off have received a wide range of assistance—not infrequently allowing them to encroach further upon the land of the poor. Support for agricultural expansion has not led to Rural Development, and it has not eliminated rural poverty. The relatively undynamic performance of many small-scale farmers under these circumstances is frequently taken as "proof" that they are a poor investment. This is a variant of "blaming the victim". In fact, the poor have fared badly, not because they could not efficiently use support, but because they did not get it.

In other words, the failure of the poor to benefit from agricultural sector investments has not reflected an economic failure among the poor themselves. Rather, it has involved policy and institutional failures. On the policy level, it has tended to reflect an unwillingness to restrain the socially influential from seeking to monopolize scarce resources to their own benefit—and, perhaps, a lack of awareness of the incompatibility between apparently "neutral" criteria for support (*e.g.*, the demand for land title as collateral for credit) and the particular circumstances of poor and small farmers (*e.g.*, involvement in traditional forms of land tenure). On the institutional level, it has involved both unwillingness to give weight to the requirements of the poor, and a lack of initiative in solving real problems in providing services to the poor such as the high cost of providing services on an individual basis to a large number of small and often dispersed "clients". While there has been a great deal of lamentation about poverty in India, remarkably little has been done to change it at the level of economic systems—perhaps because social welfare activities are much easier to implement than real policy and institutional changes. It is possible to do very much better—not by simply pouring in more resources (in channels which at times do not even ultimately reach the poor), but by changing the framework of investment, *i.e.*, the instruments of development.

LESSONS LEARNED

Targeting of Resources

The fundamental lessons learned are that investment resources must be targeted at the poor. In a world of competition for scarce resources, investments in rural development tend to be captured by those with national and local power—a group which rarely encompasses the rural poor. The first step in delivering resources to the poor is establishing strict criteria for eligibility for assistance. Indicators of wealth in India vary according to the nature of the local economy—in some cases it is extent of land ownership, in others size of cattle herds, in yet others ownership of draught animals—but the principle remains the same investment in those with the least assets. In some cases, for example, where women represent a significant proportion of actual producers, this may give rise to entirely new patterns of investment.

Reorienting Institutions

The intention to distribute resources to the poorest is not always accompanied by actual performance. Among the reasons for this is the inappropriateness of delivery mechanisms. Put simply, institutions long oriented to the non-poor have tended to develop operating procedures and structures which reflect the nature of their *de facto* clientele and which hinder them from serving a new target group. In the area of credit, for example, insistence upon collateral in land may be an absolute obstacle to participation by the poor—just as a limited banking network may represent an obstacle to delivery to the poor, for whom the costs of communicating with a bank at considerable distance might well add significantly to the real cost of credit. Effectively channelling resources to the poor, therefore, means the elaboration of institutional means of delivery consistent with their circumstances.

However, it must be recognized that there are exceptional institutional costs associated with providing services to (and among) the poor—costs arising from the fact that there are many individuals involved, and that their individual requirements tend to be quite small. The costs of Government services in, for example, agricultural credit, are necessarily higher if this involves a very large number of small producers than if it involves a small number of large producers. Administration costs in banking tend to be much higher relative to loan volume if it involves a myriad of individual small loans. These factors have often been adduced as reasons for the "impossibility" of serving the poor. Effective Service appears financially impossible, especially the context of widespread retrenchment in public expenditure under structural adjustment programmes. The poor are often willing to pay the actual costs of services—especially if the alternative is no service at all, or supply by local informal monopolists. On the other hand, there are proven ways of reducing costs of service supply to the poor—by involving the poor themselves. Everywhere in India poor people overcome some of the obstacles involved in their individual poverty through cooperation and joint action. While such organization typically develops in the absence of formal service organizations and markets, it can also develop in association with formal organizations. In effect, the organized small farmers can help shoulder the cost of services through organizing local level distribution and administration themselves.

People's Participation

People's participation is, therefore, not only a "social" concept. It is an eminently economic concept, involving cost sharing. It is fundamental to the sustainability of improvements. The long-term solution is not to throw money at the problems of the poor, but to help them to organize to overcome them themselves. One of the happy externalities of this approach is not only lower cost services, but services more likely to be in harmony—with what small farmers perceive themselves as needing.

Balanced Development

Development means change, not only in the volume of production, but in the composition of output and the conditions under which it is produced. What is argued is that the pursuit of development without the inclusion of the mass of small-scale producers and the poor has important structural drawbacks, and that their inclusion offers the basis for more sustainable long-term development. Some smallholder groups have a vast unutilized potential for expansion. Others have much more modest prospects.

Even those with the poorest assets and possibilities, however, can be helped to improve their condition. While the direct economic benefits of this maybe relatively slender, the side-effects may be great. An eventual shift of these groups to other areas and systems of production might be inevitable if aspirations for a better life are to be satisfied, but it is essential that this shift be orderly necessitating that support be given in the transitional period. This support can be either a direct welfare transfer or an investment in productive capacity. In many cases the latter may be the least-cost alternative.

The issue, then, is neither the "rich way" nor the "poor way". What is required is: an unprejudiced evaluation of the capacities and possibilities of poor and small-scale producers, and their potential role in the overall scheme of national development; allocation of investment resources according to potential and within an institutional framework ensuring delivery and profitable use; and a more balanced view of the overall social costs and benefits of alternative means of addressing transitional states. The belief is that the outcome of this will involve a reappraisal of the role of the poor in Economic Development, and a major improvement in the state of the 'rural poor throughout India.

The poor are many, their productive potential is great, but in few places is the exploitation of this potential an explicit focus of policy concern and action—although, everywhere it is the concern of the poor themselves. While concrete evidence of the efficacy of systematic policy of support to the poor is sparse (simply because it has so rarely been tried), the evidence of its effectiveness on the local level is abundant.

29

RURAL POVERTY IN INDIA

"It is morning in a remote farming area in India. As her husband harnesses a bullock to plough their field, a woman pounds the grain she will use for the day's main meal. Three kilometres away, their children are collecting fuel wood and water before starting their morning walk to school".

"After school, they help their mother light a fire with a few sticks, milk the cow and collect the sundried grain. That evening, as 'the family rests around the hearth, father worries about how to sell his onions before they spoil and the price falls. Before sleeping, his wife prepares a basket of home-grown vegetables to sell next day at the village market five kilometres away. With the takings, she hopes to buy a kerosene lamp although she might not have enough cash left to buy the kerosene immediately...."

That description of rural-life is a daily reality for hundreds of millions of families throughout India. Rural poverty 1990s means subsistence on the meagre earnings of wage labour or unreliable harvests from small plots of land. It means raising a family without safe drinking water or proper sanitation, suffering disease or injury without medical assistance. In times of unemployment or crop failure, it means living with the pangs of hunger—and the risk of death by famine.

INSIDE THE POVERTY TRAP

Poverty in Rural India is created and perpetuated by a number of closely interlinked socio-economic processes:

1. Policies and institutional arrangements biased against the poor exclude them from the benefits of development, frustrate their productive potential and accentuate the impact of other poverty processes.

   Institutional processes that perpetuate rural poverty include lack of access to land, inequitable share- cropping and tenancy arrangements, poor markets, limited access to credit, inputs and technology, and ineffective extension services. Other constraints are lack of training facilities, inadequate research related to smallholder farming systems, and last but not least—a lack of grassroots institutions needed to foster people's participation.

   Policy and institutional biases have short and long-term impacts. In the-short-term, the poor are unable to earn enough to meet nutritional requirements or to take advantage of the market. "In the longer term", "poor households continue to lag behind because they do not generate a surplus for investment, nor do they have access to investment opportunities. Moreover, the rural poor may be forced to overuse resources, which undermines productivity, and

2. Even today dualistic agrarian structures originating in colonial times persist. In India, highly capitalized large and medium-sized farms have virtually monopolistic control over land and labour, at the expense of the small farm sector. Large scale commercial producers—control the best farm land. Resources have been funnelled into irrigated plantations producing cotton and mechanized cultivation of sorghum. In marginal areas, mechanization has led to environmental degradation and the loss of seasonal grazing and stock routes for pastoralists.

   "Thus, side by side with modern agriculture, millions of marginal farmers and herdsmen subsist far below the poverty line". This dualism severely limits their capacity to grow food and accumulate capital. They lack marketable surpluses, and incentives and opportunities to save and invest.

3. Rapid population growth can cause and perpetuate rural poverty by increasing pressure on limited productive resources, social services and employment, as well as—paradoxically—creating labour shortages through outmigration.

   The most obvious consequence of rapid population growth is that, even with relatively high rates of economic growth, improvements in living conditions are limited. Total saving in the economy declines, leaving fewer resources for investment in human development. Negative consequences are most acute in rural areas. Growing population often combined with traditional laws of inheritance—has led to fragmentation of holdings, degradation of crop and pasture land, and falling yields. In areas with unequal distribution of land, rapid population growth has accelerated proletarization of the rural work force and reduced incomes.

4. Rural poverty malnutrition and under-nutrition are closely linked to environmental degradation. Poor people in marginal areas are destroying natural resources as they struggle to keep their production systems sustainable. In acute shortage of arable land has forced farmers to reduce the length of fallow periods and plough up land previously reserved for grazing. These practices have led to declining yields, soil depletion and further impoverishment. Population pressure is pushing weaker members of the rural community into ecologically vulnerable areas.

   Degradation of the environment is strongly linked to household food insecurity and lack of fuel. Much of the fragile forest cover has been destroyed by poor rural people in the search for grazing land and fuel wood.

   Government policies have also wrought environmental damage. A rapid expansion of areas under crops often accelerates deforestation and land degradation. Programmes to expand cereal production into marginal areas, subsidized capital to support commercial operations subsidies for inappropriate technologies and excessive transfer of income out of the agricultural sector may undermine the sustainability of small-holders and pastoralists' production systems.

Inadequate public investment in off-farm employment and infrastructure, a lack of price incentives and inadequate access to modern agricultural inputs and services discourage investment in land conservation, leading to further overuse and degradation.

5. As poverty undermines traditional social bonds, the marginalization of women has become a fact of rural life in India. With little or no access to land, millions of women depend on casual employment on meagre wages. Often, they farm fragmented plots of poor quality. Limited access to inputs, extension, training and credit limits, in turn, their ability to enter commercial agriculture.

   The exodus of males in search of work in Urban Areas (itself an indicator of poverty) has serious consequences for the women they leave behind. Output from land often falls and less attention is paid to maintenance, setting the stage for a long-term decline in productivity. Many female headed households have abandoned the use of oxen for ploughing, some plough and plant late and others no longer weed their fields.

6. The ethnic or cultural marginalization of tribal or minority populations also plays a role in poverty. Many of these groups are further threatened by newly marginalized groups—as the expansion of cultivation reduces the grazing areas of nomadic herders.

7. Exploitative middle-men also perpetuate rural poverty. Landlords exploit share croppers and tenants, moneylenders exploit debtors, and traders exploit small scale producers. During seasonal food shortages, the poor may have to borrow money at interest rates

exceeding 20 per cent a month. Forced to devote most of their energies to debt servicing, they sink deeper into the poverty trap.

In some cases, Government controlled cooperatives and Government agencies whose task is to protect the poor may themselves practise forms of exploitation. Heavy levies imposed by Government agencies have damaged small farmers. Large, inefficient bureaucracies are paid for by the productive sectors of the community and frequently contribute to the accumulation of large budget deficits.

8. Political troubles and civil strife have had a disastrous impact on the rural poor one effect is the disruption of development assistance to the rural poor, both from national and international agencies Another is the transformation of many producers into consumers of social services, with serious consequences for production, savings, capital accumulation and investment.
9. The international economic environment directly influences the well-being of the Indian poor. Falling commodity prices and protectionist policies in India affect the employment and incomes of plantation workers and small-holders producing for export, particularly those relying heavily on a few agricultural commodities. Changes in international interest rates have repeatedly hurt small-scale producers in debt-burdened India, while world grain price increases has triggered rural famines.

The net flow of development resources to agriculture also affects rural poverty. Official development funding for food and agriculture increased between 1975 and 1982, but has fluctuated irregularly since. Moreover, concern with trade balances is diverting resources to export crops, sometimes at the expense of traditional crops grown by poor farmers.

30

THE STATUS OF SAVING

National savings rates have been declining for several years in many countries of the industrial and developing world. Given the importance of saving to the global economy, this trends is causing much concern. Saving is critical to maintain growth and to help solve the problem of international debt. Declining saving rates have been associated with lower rates of capital accumulation and slower growth in the global economy. Moreover, differing rates of saving among countries have contributed to the emergence of large trade imbalances.

Most economies agree that if these long-run trends continue, they would have a serious impact on International Economic Growth. Yet attention has recently shifted to the potential consequences of a more immediate threat—that of a short-run global capital shortage. There are claims that this is caused by increase demands on global financial resources resulting from such events as the process of transition in Eastern Europe and the former Soviet Union, German unification, reconstruction of the Middle-East, disaster relief, and structural support of countries in debt. At the same time, large private and public sector deficits persist in important industrial countries. Even countries like Germany and Japan are experiencing a decline in their traditional surpluses of capital because of structural changes in their economies.

These factors mean that World Capital Markets are likely to become increasingly competitive. Countries needing capital in both North and South may face scarcer supplies of funds. Can the perceived shortage of global savings be avoided? Do the world's financial markets have the capacity to absorb additional demands for funds? Can structural changes in the global economy take place in the global economy take place in a way that does not jeopardize growth? Or, will a savings shortage perpetuate high interest rates (or even increase them) and limit economic growth?

TRENDS IN SAVING

Global savings and investment are notoriously difficult to measure. The latest reliable estimate puts total world saving at approximately US $ 5.2 Trillion in 1995. On a global scale, both saving and investment have declined as a percentage of the Gross National Product (GNP) since the early 1980s.

Since the mid-1980s, the OECD countries have become net importers of capital. All over the world, and particularly in North America and a few other industrial countries, Government debt generates a demand for money. OPEC countries provided most of the financial resources needed by world markets during the 1980s. But since the downturn in oil prices hit the OPEC region in 1983, newly industrializing countries in Asia (and particularly Taiwan) have largely take over this role. About 80 per cent of total private saving is accumulated In the industrial world. In the Developing World. Africa has consistently suffered from insufficient saving, although the situation has improved slightly during the 1960s. More recently, Asian and Latin American Countries have become excess savers.

GLOBAL BALANCE

For an individual country, or even a region, imbalances between savings and investment are not necessarily critical. A country can invest more that it saves and borrow what it needs on capital markets. Countries that are excess savers supply the necessary funds. On a global scale, however, the supply of savings must equal the demand for investment. In other words, one country's investment must be another country's savings.

But the global balance between planned saving and desired investment can be lopsided. For example, greater demands for investment will trigger processes of adjustment; either the price of borrowing capital will rise (*i.e.*, higher interest rates) or certain investment projects will not be funded. Capital shortages largely affect world markets through higher interest rates. Indeed, world interest rates did rise during the 1980s and the early 1990s. The 1980s have in fact been quite atypical, in that real (meaning corrected for inflation) interest rates have persisted at unprecedented levels, possibly as a result of greater demands on world financial markets. Competing economic theories have identified a number of potential culprits for this enduring increase. An insufficient amount of savings (either current or expected) is only one of many hypotheses explaining the rise in real interest rates.

REDUCED DEMAND

The unification of Germany, the Transitional Economies of Eastern Europe and the Commonwealth of Independent States, reconstruction of the Middle East, and new lending to developing countries account for about a 3 per cent increase in demand for world savings. There are, however, trends in other areas that appear to signal a reduced need for funds. For example, investment has slowed in the previously booming commercial real estate markets in the United States and elsewhere. Moreover, there are indications that the rates of fixed investment in Japan during the 1980s are not likely to be sustained.

The possibility also exists for more savings in the pubic sector industrial countries. These range from prospects for tax increases in Germany to massive reductions in military expenditures, particularly in the US. The rapid advancement of European integration is likely to lead to improved fiscal discipline and consolidated budgets, and thus reduced public sector spending. At any rate, Government deficits are still critical and reducing them will be important for future national saving in industrial countries.

Private saving behaviour is difficult to project in that it reflects a society's values and changing preferences. The latest medium-term International Monetary Fund forecast, however, show that private savings in industrial countries will drop by about 0.5 per cent of GNP, primarily because of a rapidly aging population and the corresponding increase in the ratio of dependants to wage earners in Japan and many European Countries.

Although, world saving might be insufficient over the short- and medium-term, it is also evident that even small changes in the current economic environment and in public and private sector behaviour could generate enough funds to eliminate the problem entirely. A first conclusion is, therefore, that forecasts of a major saving gap or an imminent capital shortfall should be treated with some sceptism. Consequently, concerns that insufficient saving wilt lead to increases in world real interest rates are also mostly unwarranted.

CREDIT SQUEEZE

Claims on world financial resources are likely to squeeze the amount of capital available from multilateral development banks and bilateral institutions to many small Developing Countries. This rationing of financial support may be as important for this group of countries as the potential eroding of the favourable terms of international lending. Small adjustments to the level of support can translate into significant setbacks for the most vulnerable countries.

Any globally co-ordinated scheme to give financial aid to selected regions must include safeguards so that the smallest, least developed, and highly indebted countries still have access to the finite sources of capital available to international agencies.

Why should individual countries be concerned about the global supply of funds, when, in the long-run, growth for any country is financed out of domestic saving? There is little evidence to suggest that the degree of access to external funds affects medium-term growth-rates in developing countries. In fact, during the last two decades, economic growth was generally lower in the Developing Countries that borrowed than in those that did not. This was largely due to the high interest-rates of the 1980s suffered by severely indebted countries. Even earlier, however, borrowers' growth rates were only marginally higher than those of non-borrowers. Although, the borrowed funds helped boost per-capita income. It is less likely that they stimulated the economies of the recipient countries. Differences in the developing countries' growth have largely been the result of differences in their rates of domestic saving. Form this perspective, national saving should be encouraged.

FEARS UNFOUNDED

A tentative conclusion is that fears of a global capital shortage, skyrocketing real Interest rates, and negative effects resulting from greater demands on international financial resources over the next few years are most likely unfounded. There appears to be as many trends pointing toward *increases in saving as there are indications of additional capital needs.* Also, even if substantial savings shortfalls were to materialize, the limited rise in real interest rates would have relatively benign effects on countries of both North and South. The only major caveat relates to small developing countries that have in the past depended upon favourable terms of lending from muiti—and bilateral institutions. If international capital shortages translate into even the smallest encroachment on the allocation of funds to these countries, their medium-term development could be threatened. In addition, the debt burdens of many developing countries suggest that in the long-run, external sources of funds cannot substitute for sufficient national saving. If domestic saving corresponds to development needs in the South, developing countries should not suffer as a result of increased competition for international capital.

Finally, while the short-term fears of a global capital shortage are clearly unwarranted, concerns about the medium-term trends in world saving are not National saving rates must be raised substantially throughout the world to allow real interest rates to decline to the post-war average of 1-1.5 per cent. That, more than anything else, will contribute to a stable expansion of the global economy.

31

WHO IS RESPONSIBLE FOR CORRUPTION IN AID?

World Bank President James Wolfensohn's pronouncement that the 'Cancer' of corruption seriously undermines development and will not be tolerated in future Bank Funded Projects prompts one to ask: where and when did this corruption originate? How much corruption is acceptable to the World Bank and donor community? For many years the World Bank tended to ignore or discount the significance of corruption in its operations. Donor agencies in general seem to have a very high tolerance for the misuse of their money. Now that the Bank, the UK system, and bilateral agencies are under growing pressure to improve their performance, they are seeking ways to limit the corrupt use of aid money. For the moment, there is little or no evidence that they have any idea of how to go about the task.

One of the main reasons for the disappointing performance of structural adjustment programmes is the misuse of donor money, including systematic corruption. An extreme example is Tanzania's import support programme, which allowed local manufacturers and traders to import raw-materials and finished goods. An increasing number of companies, both private and parastatal, began to abuse the system. They stopped paying counterpart funds. Import duty and sales tax were not paid on imports. Neither, the Treasury nor the commercial banks had the administrative capacity or the integrity to handle large volumes of free foreign exchange, but the donors ignored the problem. Only when the scandalous behaviour of the Banks, the Treasury and the Minister of Finance had reached epic proportions, fuelling inflation and completely derailing the budgetary process, did the World Bank and other donors finally pull the plug on import support.

In December 1996, the IMF started disbursing US $ 240 million enhanced structural adjustment loan, but to date not one private or parastatal company has been put in receivership for the hundreds of millions of donor dollars which went astray via import support. This casual approach to large-scale corruption has been the norm among donors.

Some bilateral donors have cut the number of countries which they assist, and eradicated funds to those remaining. To increase aid effectiveness some of them have also reduced the number of sectors they support per country. Add to this the tendency for the whole donor community to move into new activities at the same time, and you have a recipe for too much aid chasing too little 'absorptive capacity' in the countries of concentration. Which include Tanzania, Uganda and Kenya, Pressure to spend has led to unbelievable over-funding in certain sectors. Well known examples are NGO's, many of which are created with the sole objective of embezzling donor money.

With the coming of political pluralism, a growing volume of aid money has been channelled into 'governance' activities. The disadvantages of governance from the donor perspective are that donors have little experience in this field, and the amounts of money which can be disbursed, compared to the amount of administrative work involved, are relatively trival.

Aid has served to encourage the establishment of a whole range of corrupt activities in 'Civil Society' to add to those which already existed in the state apparatus. Many of those managing the corruption are recent migrants from the state sector, or straddle both public and private sectors. The politically acceptable employment of more local personnel as desk officers has served to increase the rate of corruption. The chances of being caught or punished are minimal. The few genuine local change-agents are crowded out by the charlatans and opportunists. The imperative to disburse at all costs makes it very difficult for donors to adequately monitor or evaluate the quality of their assistance, since it would put the agencies in a poor light if they were seen to be supporting non-performing and corrupt activities. Thus, as has generally been the case, the donors pretend that their assistance is being well used, and are even prepared to deny well founded allegations of the misuse of project funds.

The new aid activities discussed above account for a relatively small proportion of total aid flows, however, the basic issue is the amount of uncontrolled corruption which still characterises the World Bank and other donors' more traditional project, programme, and financial support. Here too one finds projects of ever growing magnitude, as the big spending goes on. The continued availability of donor money is the major determinant of the volume of aid, not performance, structural reform, or impact on 'target groups'. Although, further project aid cannot be justified on the basis of past performance, it continues to be a major form of aid delivery by both the World Bank and other donor agencies.

The picture which emerges is that of an oppressed people largely at the mercy of an incompetent and corrupt state apparatus. The role of aid in helping to create and reproduce this lamentable state of affairs is worth exploring. Unfortunately, the report does riot mention corruption in aid. If corruption has become one of the major international issues of modern times, it would hardly be surprising to find that the virus has already infected and is spreading within the major agencies.

If countries with as much corruption as Tanzania, Uganda, and Kenya can continue to enjoy billions of dollars of aid every year, it is not because they have demonstrated their ability to use aid wisely. But the donors are not well placed to extol the virtues of transparency and accountability which they do not practice themselves. To address the question of corruption in aid, the World Bank and other agencies will have to take a long look at their own role in creating the problem which they now propose to cure.

32

FINANCE MATTERS

(Financial Liberalisation: Too Much Too Soon)

An efficient and stable Financial System is important for economic growth and poverty reduction. The financial crises that have afflicted many countries in recent times have been a costly and painful reminder of the disastrous consequences for development of weak financial markets. The recurrence of financial crises, at both the international and national levels, and the adverse effect they have had on economic growth and poverty levels, have highlighted the need for a policy framework which addresses the inherent vulnerability of financial markets to systemic instability and failure.

Governments have always intervened in the financial sector and there are sound theoretical and practical reasons for doing so. Financial markets are characterised by problems of limited and unequal information, making them inherently imperfect and prone to failure. Financial regulation and supervision are therefore, essential for efficient and stable financial market development. How should Governments intervene? Have financial liberalisation and financial sector reform made financial systems more, or less vulnerable to instability and systemic crises? How can the process be better managed? What is the best policy framework for supporting financial sector development in low-income countries.

REPRESSION TO LIBERALISATION

For many years, Governments followed a policy of financial 'repression', which relied on fixing interest rates below market levels and controlling the allocation of credit. The economic distortions induced by these policies were considerable. Financial systems remained under-developed, lending patterns were inefficient and failed to achieve their distributional goals. Negative real interest rates led to low-savings and encouraged capital flight. Macro-economic performance also deteriorated countries with large negative real interest rates experienced lower allocation efficiency and growth rates. In the state owned banking sector, poor lending decisions (often politically influenced) and low repayment rates led to bank insolvency and large budgetary bailouts of depositors and creditors.

A growing awareness of the economic costs of financial 'repression', led to financial 'liberalisation' as the dominant policy paradigm over the past two decades. Initially, the relaxation of controls on interest rates was the focus for financial reform which was often triggered by a financial crisis. The relaxation of controls on the financial sector was often part of a more general policy shift towards liberalisation of the domestic economy and opening upto the international economy liberalisation soon broadened therefore, beyond interest rate liberalisation, to include a wide range of measures constituting a programme of financial sector reform was adopted under World Bank sectoral or structural adjustment lending conditionalities, the key elements of which included privatisation of banks, entry of new domestic and foreign entrants into the banking sector, bank restructuring and recapitalisation, opening upto the capital account, strengthening bank regulation and supervision institutions.

HAS FINANCIAL LIBERALISATION WORKED

The period of financial liberalisation coincided with, or was soon followed by heightened financial instability, culminating in the dramatic financial crisis in East Asia in the second-half of the 1990s. Clearly, financial liberalisation has not led to a smooth transition to a stable and efficient financial system. It would be wrong, however, to jump to the easy, but shallow, conclusion that financial liberalisation has 'failed'. Firstly, the fact that the period of increased systemic instability does not prove causality. Secondly, no process of change comes cheap: a reasoned assessment of the costs and benefits of the policy change is needed. And thirdly, what would have been the outcome without the policy change" Finally the impact of financial liberalisation will differ between countries, depending on each country's economic and institutional characteristics. The more relevant research issue, therefore, relates to the design and timing of context-specific policy measures, which will contribute to the development of an efficient and stable financial system. Could financial liberalisation have been managed better? If so, what policies are now needed? The commercial banks are the dominant component of the financial sector in low-income countries and are critical to the efficiency and stability of the financial system as a whole. Financial liberalisation was associated with a shift in prudential regulation from direct regulation of banks, by for example, regular site visits, to an indirect approach based on the monitoring of bank capital to ensure that it remained adequate in relation to the risk being taken. Additional regulatory measures are also necessary to restrain the activities of the privatised and other newly—established private banks. The regulatory and supervisory frame-work may also need to be extended, to cover micro-finance institutions which have developed significant deposit taking capacity.

Four main obstacles to efficient banking regulations are:

(a) information, contracting and monitoring problems,

(b) lack of supervisory personnel,

(c) high operational costs, and

(d) poor credibility and regulation of regulatory bodies. The appropriateness of various-policy measures for dealing with these constraints are discussed and ranked in terms of their suitability for low-income countries. What are the implications of allowing micro-finance institutions to offer a range of financing services beyond small-scale lending.

TOO MUCH, TOO SOON?

The experience with financial liberalisation reveals a strong correlation between liberalisation and financial crisis. This can be explained partly by the exposure of existing inefficiencies and distortions in the financial structure, and partly by a failure to develop a strong regulatory and supervisory framework, prior to liberalisation. Weakness in the initial conditions affect the ability of the privatised banks and new market entrants, to operate on broadly commercial principles. Borrowers are often unable to service their loans, due to poor quality lending and high interest rates. Liberalisation of the capital account increases the inflow of foreign capital, but at the same time threatens that stability of the financial institutions by increasing the exchange-rate and domestic lending risks.

The existing regulatory and supervisory system may be unsuited to a market-based environment. Consequently, across the board 'big-bang' financial liberalisation and financial sector reform increase the likelihood of systemic crisis, where the institutional and human resource environment is weak. Much of the blame for post-liberalisation financial crisis lies, therefore, with the scale and sequencing of financial reform. What is needed is a more gradual and considered approach to financial liberalisation, which recognises that institutional strengthening, especially in the regulation and supervision capacity, is a prerequisite and supervision capacity is a prerequisite for creating a more efficient and stable financial sector which can contribute fully to achieving economic growth and poverty reduction in developing countries.

BIBLIOGRAPHY

Anand, P.P., *Legal Regime of Sea Bed and the Developing Countries*, 1975.

Bhatt, S., *Environment Protection and International Law*, Radiant Publication, Kalkaji, New Delhi, 1985, pp. 122.

—*Environmental Laws and Water Resources Management*, Radiant Publication, India, and Advent Books Inc. New York, 1986, pp. 355.

Behrman, Danial, *In Partnership with Nature*—UNESCO and the Environment (Paris, 1973).

Bell, Daniel, "Technology, Nature and Society", *American Scholar*, Summer 1973.

Bentley, Glass, "Biology and Human Values", USIS, New Delhi.

Book of Nature: *The Way Things Work*, Published by George Allen and Unwin Ltd., 1981, pp. 525.

Boulding, Kenneth E., "New Goals for Society", S.H. Schun, ed., *Energy, Economic Growth and the Environment*.

Carr, E.H., *What is History*, 1961.

Darlington, C.D., *The Evolution of Man and Society* (London, 1961).

Downing, Paul B., ed., *Air Pollution and Social Sciences* (New York, 1971).

"Drive to Adopt National Water Policy". *Times of India*, 22 July, 1983.

Dubos, Rene, "Man and His Environment", *Britannica Perspectives*, Vol. 1, 1968.

Einstein, A., *My Views*, ed. by S.K. Bandopadhyaya (Calcutta, 1976).

"Environment Research Programme", prepared by NCEPC, Department of Science and Technology, New Delhi.

Forbes, R.J., "The Conquest of Nature and its Consequences", *Britannica Perspectives*, Vol. 1, 1968.

Fowler, John M., *Energy and Environment* (New York, 1975).

Fuller, Buckminister R., *Operating Manual for Spaceship Earth* (New York, 1969).

Gandhi, Indira, "Poverty Greatest Pollution, Says Mrs. Gandhi", *Times of India*, 8 September, 1981.

Glenn, Seaborg, "Science, Technology and Development: A New World Outlook", USIS, New Delhi.

Hacoley, Amos H., *Human Ecology* (New York, 1950).

"India Must Develop Own Ecology". *Times of India*, 8 October. 1981.

Marion, Jerry B., *Energy in Perspective* (London, 1974).

Misra, K.C., *Manual of Plant Ecology*, New Delhi, 1980.

Mukherji, P.K., *Life of Tagore, trans*, by S.K. Ghosh, 1975.

Mumford, Lewis, "The Future of Cities", in *Basic Issues in Environment*, E.J. Whin, ed., 1972.

Palmslierna, H., *Future Imperatives for Human Environment*, 1972.

Pavithran, A.K., "World Futurology", *Eastern Journal of International Law* (Madras), vol. 9.

"Plans to Usher India into 21st Century", *Times of India*, 24 October, 1985.

Polunin, Nicholas, "The Biosphere Today", *The Environmental Future*, Proceedings of 1st International Conference on Environmental Future in Finland, ed. by N. Polunin, 1972.

Radhakrishnan, S., *Recovery of Faith*, 1967.

Report on the State of Environment Prepared by Centre for Science and Environment, New Delhi, 1985.

Sarkar, Mahendra Nath, *The Cultural Heritage of India*, Vol. 1.

Sen, Sudhir, "Blueprint for a Better World", *Times of India*, 2 March, 1980.

The Limits to Growth, a Report to Club of Rome (New York, 1972).

The Mind of J. Krishnamurti, ed. by L.S.R. Vas (Bombay, 1971).

Toynbee, Arnold, "Man and His Soul", *Hindustan Times*, 4 January, 1968.

iteUnd Nations List of National Parks and Protected Areas, 1985.

Vivekananda, Swami, *Complete Works*, Vol. II (Calcutta, 1968).

Ward, Barbara and Dubos Rene, *Only one Earth: The Care and Maintenance of a Small Planet*. Report to UN Conference on Human Environment, Stockholm, 1972.

"Wildlife Laws in India", *Times of India*, 4 March, 1985.

Ward, Barbara, *Progress for a Small Planet*, 1979.

INDEX